Photo credits:

Soldiers and helicopter on air assault mission- May 14, 2007.
Photo courtesy of U.S. Army and taken by unknown
photographer.

Business model review. Photo purchased from Jupiterimages.

Family praying together at dinner. Photo purchased from
Istockphoto.

Family watching a movie. Photo purchased from Jupiterimages.

Basketball photo of Kent State/Bowling Green game on February
24, 2004. Photo courtesy of U.S. Army and taken by Jeff
Glidden.

Baseball photo of Stuttgart/Wiesbaden Bulldogs winning German
Little League title, July, 2007. Photo courtesy of U.S. Army.
Photographer unknown.

Thank You

I would like to thank a few special people that helped make this book possible.

LTG(R) Peter Kind and COL(R) Archie B. Taylor, two of the wisest men I have had the pleasure to learn from. Thank you for sharing your wisdom with me over the years and for being exceptional role models to me and to many.

Joshua B. Creson, my best friend and my brother. You are a tremendous leader and father, whom I have learned much from over the years. I so look forward to our talks about leadership, family, and God and applying the lessons learned to real life. Thank you for helping to bring this book from concept to reality.

Dave Pindell. A tremendous leader in your own right. We have watched each other transform from young men without a clue to men trying to do what is right. I admire your convictions and am honored to call you friend. I thank you for your masterful edits and insightful comments which transformed this book into a helpful guide.

Mom, Tricia, and Kathleen. Thank you for your inspiration, love, patience, and support as I worked through this endeavor. I am truly blessed to have each one of you in my life and my life is much richer due to each of you.

25 Days to becoming a Better Leader at Work, Home, and Play

Foreword

Leadership.

     This book is designed to provide the reader with some general concepts on how you can become a better leader at work, home, and play. "25 Days to becoming a Better Leader at Work, Home, and Play" is specifically written for people new to leadership roles, but what it teaches is also applicable as a reminder to any person serving in any leadership position.

     The intended reading format is to read one chapter a day, reflect on it, and then apply the principles to one's life. Almost every chapter begins with a situation most will be able to relate to in some shape or form. From there, I point out some different leadership principles/thoughts/management techniques and then I close with some questions for the reader to think about.

     Even though each chapter is written as a stand alone chapter for study, leadership is dynamic. Therefore, many fo the principles discussed in this book will build upon principles learned/ discussed in previous chapters. Furthermore, leadership is not a one time speech or event. Leadership is an every day service to perform and practice. That is right-leadership is a service. Great leaders recognize this point and act accordingly.

     It is my desire that after reading this book the reader will apply these principles and continue to grow as a leader at work, home, and play. The choice is up to you. Being a great leader is demanding, but well worth the sacrifices.

Chapter 1

Are You Part of the Problem or Part of the Solution?

Situation 1, Car analogy

I was driving down the road the other day with a passenger in the front seat of my car. There were a few cars in front of me, to the right of me, and behind me. I was about four car lengths behind the car in front of me when I briefly took my eyes off the road and glanced into the rear view mirror to check the vehicle behind me.

Then, all of a sudden, I saw a blur to the right of me so I looked at my passenger; she had thrown her hands up in front of her face! I immediately looked to the front and saw that the guy in the car in front of me had made a split second decision to make a left turn and had slammed on his brakes in order to do so. To avoid him, I slammed on my brakes and looked into my mirror so I could see how the person in the car behind me was reacting. That person had stopped safely so I didn't have to let up on my brakes or try and swerve left to avoid a three car accident. Fortunately, there wasn't any accident, but I did glean a great leadership principle.

Was my passenger part of the problem or part of the solution? She saw the problem ahead and threw her hands up. She did nothing to prevent the accident. In the above situation, my passenger was part of the problem. Had my passenger been proactive and yelled, "Stop!" and then braced for impact, my passenger would have been part of the solution. I would have immediately slammed on the brakes and had an even better chance of avoiding an accident. By bracing for impact, my passenger would have been thinking one step in the future and been able to minimize injury to herself.

Let's apply this to the workplace. How often do you hear someone badmouthing the leadership, but not providing any solutions to better the situation? How about your coworker or yourself complaining about everything, but doing nothing to fix it? Does it sound familiar? Are you part of the problem or part of the solution?

Instead of just being a complainer, why don't you or you and your workers think of a better way to perform the process that isn't where it needs to be? Now, you are part of the solution. But don't stop there. While you are trying to solve this problem make sure you identify what the real problem is. A real leader has to be able to tell the difference between problems vs. symptoms. We will tackle that topic in the next chapter.

Back to my car analogy. Even though I did not hit the car in front of me and the car behind me did not run into me, should I as a leader just accept what happened and pretend it did not? No! I need to evaluate what happened and correct the problem so it doesn't happen in the future. Although there are numerous ways to approach this, here is how I chose to correct the problem.

For myself, I recognized the fact that I need to make sure I pay closer attention to the road and make the checks to the rear a little shorter in length. For my passenger, I told her the next time there is a situation like this, she needs to yell at me to stop (or whatever else I need to do) and not throw her hands up as it does nothing to solve the problem.

This should have been the end of the conversation, but my passenger had other ideas. She angrily and sarcastically responded, "If you can't see what is directly in front of you, how can I help?" Does this sound familiar? It is easy to be angry and complain, but that is not being part of the solution. You have to get your subordinate or coworker to calm down and think rationally. Help them to be part of the solution. In this case, I calmly told my passenger that I did make a mistake and that if we worked together in the future instead of separately we can both benefit from it. I also made some jokes, mostly at myself.

2

Situation 2, Father to son bad incident analogy

The son has made some type of bad judgment call-
stealing, sex, sports, lying, etc.

Father: "Do you know what you did? I can't believe you did
what you did! What possessed you to do that? You know
better than that! I just can't believe you did that! What do
you have to say about yourself young man?"

Son: "Well, Dad."

Father interrupting: "Son, I just can't believe you did that.
That was so stupid! I am so upset with you. What was
going through your mind that made you do something as
stupid as that?"

So Dad, are you part of the problem or part of the
solution? Does berating your son fix the behavior? No, it just
makes your child tune you out and inflames an already bad
situation. Dad, you are part of the problem. Tell your child you
are disappointed once and then move on to how to correct the
problem behavior (See Chapter 6, Discipline).

Situation 3, Coach to player

"Justin, you are playing like crap. Go warm the bench!" or
"Get your butt off my court! You can't play basketball to
save your life!"

Coach, are you part of the problem or part of the
solution? Maybe all you need to do is teach Justin to dribble for
a few hours or practice passing drills until Justin can do it in his
sleep. Most players need help in some specific area. Force
them to work on those skills. Maybe bench the player until he
learns the skills, but you have to identify the problem first in order
to fix it. Putting someone down and not taking the time to correct
the behavior will never solve the problem. Coach, for you to be
part of the solution, you have to show Justin how to overcome
his failure.

Situation 4, Rubbernecking

You are cruising down the highway at 65 mph enjoying life and then ahead you see traffic is backed up for what seems like miles because of an accident. After twenty minutes of now going 5 mph, you get frustrated and think, "Why does every car have to slow down, stop, and look at the accident? If they just did 25 MPH it would be safe for police, everyone else, and speed things up." But when you get to the wreck, what do you do? Slow down and stop. Are you part of the problem or part of the solution? You know what the solution is, but because you didn't implement it, you are part of the problem!

Situation 5, Sun tan lotion

Let's say you have a sun tan lotion that all the experts say is the best, but everyone you know that uses it gets a sun burn. Are you going to use it? And let's say everyone else you know uses a different sun tan lotion that the experts recommend against, but none of these friends get a sun burn. If you recommend to someone that they use the "expert" product even though you know it doesn't work, are you part of the problem or part of the solution? You are part of the problem.

Situation 6, Rumor at work, home, or play

Anyone: "The real reason Betty got a raise is...."

Anyone: "The only reason he is starting quarterback is because he is the coach's son."

Anyone: "Jason did this, Jason did that, and then Jason did..." (A complete set of lies or half-truths intended to hurt someone).

Anyone: "Did you hear about...?"

Is the spread of rumors or even listening to rumors being part of the problem or being part of the solution? Rumors destroy teams/organizations/and families. Spreading and listening to rumors is being part of the problem.

Let's apply what we have learned. In any given situation, are you part of the problem or part of the solution? What about your employees/teammates/or children? How you react and interpret situations either solves the problem or makes it worse. Evaluate yourself in some past situations. Look at how you and/or others reacted. How should you have acted? Now, how can you act/react better in the future?

Chapter 2

Identify and Fix the Problem, Not the Symptoms

Situation 1, Wet lubricant

Let's say you have a "wet" lubricant and weapon (gun) in a sandy, dusty, and dirty environment. You are given the guidance to clean your weapon eight times a day due to the environmental conditions which cause the weapon to malfunction at an unacceptably high rate.

Despite cleaning the weapon as directed, it continues to regularly malfunction. Is the problem you aren't cleaning your weapon enough? No! The problem is not with how many times you do or you don't clean your weapon. The problem is a "wet" lubricant will always attract the sand, the dust, and the dirt which will cause it to malfunction.

Cleaning the weapon more only temporarily treats the symptom. To treat the problem of a "wet" lubricant, you have to use a "dry" lubricant instead. A "dry" lubricant is "dry" to the touch so it will not attract the sand, the dust, or the dirt and weapons won't jam.

Many times leaders incorrectly identify the symptom as the problem and prescribe the wrong resource (cure) in response. Also, using the wrong resource will never generate a permanent fix to the problem and may, in fact, accelerate the problem.

Situation 2, Comedian

I remember hearing a comedian say once that his car had a problem. The muffler had a hole in it that was getting bigger every day so the muffler noise was also getting louder everyday. To avoid hearing the muffler leak, he turned up the radio; thus, presto, no problem! Isn't this what we do with a lot of our problems? We treat the symptom, not the problem!

Most of the time identifying the true problem, not treating the symptom, is as simple as asking a few more questions or running a few more tests. Let's look at a few examples.

You own a car and when it rains, water leaks in around the windshield. Does parking the car inside to prevent it from leaking during a rain storm solve the problem? No, it treats the symptom. To solve the problem, you have to replace the leaky gasket around the windshield.

If your grass has weeds and it is overgrown, will mowing the lawn get rid of the weed problem? No, mowing the lawn will just make the weeds shorter and the lawn look nicer. To solve the problem of the weeds, you must remove the weeds by pulling out their roots or using weed killer.

Your basketball team gets beat by another team, is the loss a problem or a symptom? It is a symptom. The loss is a result. What caused the result? The problem did. In this case, the problem was your team wasn't able to defend or outscore the opponent.

Note: If we drilled deeper, i.e. why was the team outscored, then being outscored is not the problem anymore, it is now the symptom of the team's play.

Your car won't start. Is that a problem or a symptom? Ok, it is a problem if you have to go somewhere right now, but for the car, strictly speaking, not starting is a symptom.

The car not starting could be because of hundreds of reasons! The ignition is bad, the battery is dead, the car is in neutral, there is water on the points, or you name it. By using a diagnostic book, you can test the different parts of the car system to identify the true problem and not treat the symptom.

Let's suppose you tested everything and found out everything is working fine, except for your battery, which is dead. Now, you have found the problem and if the battery is four years old, the probable solution is to purchase a new battery.

If, however, the battery is only two months old, then the battery being dead is only a symptom. To find the problem, you have to ask yourself what could cause an otherwise perfectly good battery to die- maybe the lights were left on or keys left in the ignition? So you look inside the car and sure enough, the headlights were left on. In this case, the real problem is you not turning off the headlights. The fix for the symptom (dead battery) is charging the battery and the fix for the problem (failure to turn the lights off) is checking to make sure the headlights are turned off before getting out of the car.

Situation 3, Personnel inprocessing

An organization I helped had a two-week personnel inprocessing timeline put in place that just wasn't doing well. Roughly 50% of the people didn't make it through the process on time and the general consensus was the process needed to change from 10 working days to 12 working days. This change would be expensive as it would increase operating costs by 50%. As it was, the current process overruns were costing the organization an extra 25%.

Everyone agreed there just wasn't enough time to get all the inprocessing done in ten days, except in exceptional cases. I didn't buy it. I asked the process leader to draw me a timeline of what happened each day and to list below each event the time it took to do the event and the limiting factor for each event (we created a flowchart). Then, I had him talk me through the timeline as I asked questions along the way. Within ten minutes of this interactive discussion, we rearranged the process resulting in a plan to complete all the tasks required for inprocessing in the current two week timeline and there was even time to spare!

So, in ten minutes, we rearranged the process and saved the organization over $1.2 million annually (cost avoidance) and it didn't cost the organization a penny! How? I identified and treated the problem (the process), not the symptom (time overrun). I asked the questions to see what was causing the time overrun. I asked "So what?" types of questions (See Chapter 20, So What?) as to why we did what we did when we did. I looked at "out of the box" solutions. Having the flowchart to look at enabled me to see the whole process (See Chapter 15, The Big Picture) and then I could look at how the parts interacted to make wise decisions.

Now, let's take what we have learned and apply it to a notional 5 day inprocessing timeline.

Here is the flowchart we began with.

5 Day Inprocessing Timeline, Unrevised

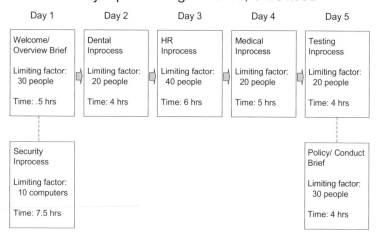

Day 1	Day 2	Day 3	Day 4	Day 5
Welcome/ Overview Brief	Dental Inprocess	HR Inprocess	Medical Inprocess	Testing Inprocess
Limiting factor: 30 people	Limiting factor: 20 people	Limiting factor: 40 people	Limiting factor: 20 people	Limiting factor: 20 people
Time: .5 hrs	Time: 4 hrs	Time: 6 hrs	Time: 5 hrs	Time: 4 hrs

Security Inprocess		Policy/ Conduct Brief
Limiting factor: 10 computers		Limiting factor: 30 people
Time: 7.5 hrs		Time: 4 hrs

5 Day Inprocessing Timeline, Unrevised

Rules Governing the process:

No one can work more than 8 hrs in a day.
Must process 20 people in 5 days.
You can not change the limiting factors.

Some questions to ask:

What is the overall limiting factor in the whole process?
What can be done before the process (Prefilled forms, etc.) to save time?
Does one process have to be done before another (i.e. order matters)?
Can people be broken up into groups?
If people can be broken up into groups, will it cut down on the process time?
Are the different stations open every day?

The first step is identifying our limiting factors. In this example, the overall limiting factor is the security process, so it is our decision point. To increase our "production," we either have to increase the number of computers, increase the number of days on the computer, and/or split up the inprocessing team from one group of twenty people to two groups of ten people or four groups of five people.

The answer to our second question, "What can be done before the process to save time?" is answered by:

Dental: Save 30 minutes by prefilling forms
Medical: Save 1 hour by prefilling forms

Does one process have to be done before another? The Welcome/Overview brief has to be the first brief. The Security inprocessing should be near the front, because if a person fails security, he goes home.

Can people be broken into groups? The answer to our question is, "We have never done it that way before." We will talk about that more in Chapter 17, Styles of Leadership. For now, we will take that answer as a "yes" and we can do it. Will it cut down on the process time if we have separate groups? Not really, only maybe five or ten minutes.

Are the different stations open every day? For the medical and dental, the answer is "no." Medical and dental can only be open for one day. For the other stations, they can be open more than one day as the employees running them are committed to this project until it is complete. That was a good question, we just found another limiting factor.

So, now our questions are answered, let's adjust our flowchart to reflect the changes.

5 Day Inprocessing Timeline, Revising

Day 1	Day 2	Day 3	Day 4	Day 5
Welcome/ Overview Brief	Dental Inprocess	HR Inprocess	Medical Inprocess	Testing Inprocess
Limiting factor: 30 people	Limiting factor: 20 people	Limiting factor: 40 people	Limiting factor: 20 people	Limiting factor: 20 people
Time: .5 hrs	Time: 4 hrs **Now: 3.5 hrs**	Time: 6 hrs	Time: 5 hrs **Now: 4 hrs**	Time: 4 hrs

Security Inprocess

Limiting factor: 10 computers

Time: 7.5 hrs

If pass, continue to inprocess

If fail, ends employment

Policy/ Conduct Brief

Limiting factor: 30 people

Time: 4 hrs

Now, let's rearrange our chart using two groups to complete the process.

5 Day Inprocessing Timeline, Group 1

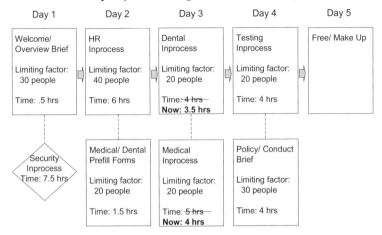

Day 1	Day 2	Day 3	Day 4	Day 5
Welcome/ Overview Brief Limiting factor: 30 people Time: .5 hrs	HR Inprocess Limiting factor: 40 people Time: 6 hrs	Dental Inprocess Limiting factor: 20 people Time: 4 hrs **Now: 3.5 hrs**	Testing Inprocess Limiting factor: 20 people Time: 4 hrs	Free/ Make Up
Security Inprocess Time: 7.5 hrs	Medical/ Dental Prefill Forms Limiting factor: 20 people Time: 1.5 hrs	Medical Inprocess Limiting factor: 20 people Time: 5 hrs **Now: 4 hrs**	Policy/ Conduct Brief Limiting factor: 30 people Time: 4 hrs	

5 Day Inprocessing Timeline, Group 2

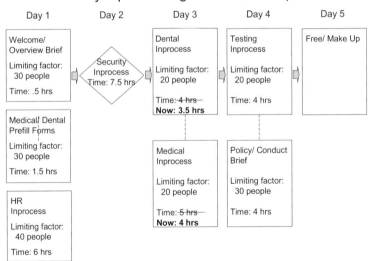

Day 1	Day 2	Day 3	Day 4	Day 5
Welcome/ Overview Brief Limiting factor: 30 people Time: .5 hrs	Security Inprocess Time: 7.5 hrs	Dental Inprocess Limiting factor: 20 people Time: 4 hrs **Now: 3.5 hrs**	Testing Inprocess Limiting factor: 20 people Time: 4 hrs	Free/ Make Up
Medical/ Dental Prefill Forms Limiting factor: 30 people Time: 1.5 hrs		Medical Inprocess Limiting factor: 20 people Time: 5 hrs **Now: 4 hrs**	Policy/ Conduct Brief Limiting factor: 30 people Time: 4 hrs	
HR Inprocess Limiting factor: 40 people Time: 6 hrs				

So, by asking a few questions and using a flowchart, we save a day in the process which translates into a 20% savings of time and money which can be used to focus on something else.

Situation 4, Tardy employee

You have an employee that has been habitually late to work the past few weeks so you set him down and say, "Jeff, you have been late a lot lately and I have counseled you about it before (See Chapter 5, Counseling and Chapter 6, Discipline). Why have you been late so much?"

Employee: "I don't know."

You: "Ok, Jeff, I am going to ask you some direct questions and I want direct answers. Why were you late today?"

Employee: "Because I got stuck in traffic."

You: "Why did you get stuck in traffic?"

Employee: "Because I had to stop for breakfast at the drive thru."

You: "Why didn't you eat breakfast at home?"

Employee: "Because I didn't have time to eat breakfast at home."

You: "Why didn't you have time to eat breakfast at home?"

Employee: "Because I only had enough time to take a shower."

You: "Why did you only have enough time to take a shower?"

Employee: "Because I got up late."

You: "Why did you get up late?"

Employee: "Because I don't have an alarm clock."

You: "Why don't you have an alarm clock?"

Employee: "Because it broke."

You: "Why didn't you replace it?"

Employee: "Because I don't have enough money to buy a new one."

You: "What do you mean? Why don't you have enough money to get an alarm clock?"

Employee: "Because I haven't got paid in two weeks and I spent all my money on bills, gas, and food and I only have $10 left."

You: "Why didn't you tell me you had a pay problem?"

Employee: "I thought you were too busy."

So, what is/are the problem(s) here? You have to keep on asking questions until you get to the root of the problem. And sometimes once you have found the root of the problem, you may need to dig even deeper because the symptoms from another problem affect the root problem. In the case above, there was a pay problem. An even worse problem exists, however, as you have an employee that doesn't feel like he can communicate with his leadership.

Situation 5, Sports

Your sports team can't perform any of their specialty plays very well and their routine play is sloppy. The symptom is their play is poor; the problem is they are not executing the basics. Go back to the basics whether it is running, ball control, pivots, one-on-one, etc. and get that right. Then, you can start doing the fancy stuff.

Situation 6, Sick

Many times when we are sick, we treat the symptoms with cold medicine. Instead, we need to attack the real problem, why did we get sick in the first place? Are you washing your hands before eating food or touching your face? Are you eating a balanced diet of healthy food? Are you drinking enough water? Are you drinking too much alcohol? Are you not getting enough rest? All of these questions center on taking care of our bodies. If we take care of our bodies in the first place, we won't get sick nearly as often when we don't take care of ourselves. Identify and treat the problem, not the symptom.

Situation 7, Family

Your son's report card has arrived in the mail and there are some failing grades.

Father: (Yelling) "Donnie, get your butt over here. You see this report card?! You see this report card?! What is your problem?"

Donnie: (Now defensive and yelling back) "It's not my fault!"

Father: (Yelling) "Not your fault? Are you just stupid or are you just trying to screw up and embarrass me? What the h*ll is your problem? You're a disgrace!"

Donnie: "I hate you!" and runs off.

Father: (Still yelling) "Get back here! I am not done with you yet." (Continues to Donnie's room and yells) "Until you get your grades up, you are grounded!"

The report card is not the problem here; it is the symptom of the problem. And the father's reaction to the report card has only compounded the problem. Let's look at this situation a different way and identify the problem.

> Father: (In a concerned, firm tone) "Donnie, I just saw your report card and you had two F's; one in English and the other in PE. I know you are smarter than that. Let's talk about your English grade first. What's going on?"

> Donnie: "I am just having a hard time understanding."

> Father: "Where do you sit in class?"

> Donnie: "In the back."

> Father: "What about other classes? Where do you sit?"

> Donnie: (A little dejected) "In the second or third row from the front."

> Father: "And let me guess. In English class, your friends sit in the back with you also."

> Donnie: "Yes."

> Father: "Do I need to have a talk with the teacher or are you going to move to the front yourself?"

> Donnie: "I will move to the front."

> Father: "Ok, how about PE what is going on there?"

> Donnie: "I haven't been dressing out."

> Father: "Why not?"

> Donnie: "I hate playing volleyball."

> Father: "That's no excuse." (Taking a deep breath and then continues) "Why do you hate volleyball?"

Donnie: "Well, I have a hard time seeing the ball and I look stupid when I miss it and everyone laughs at me."

Father: "Maybe we need to go see the eye doctor. Tell me, do you have a hard time seeing the board in English also."

Donnie: "But Dad, I don't want to wear glasses!"

Father: "I guess that answers that question. Now Donnie, I also want you to ask your teachers if anything can be done to bring up your grades. You know, extra credit. You will do the extra credit and I will help you if you need it. When you get home tomorrow, I want to hear what you have for me."

Donnie: (A questioning voice) "But Dad?"

Father: "No but's about it and because I love you I am going to make sure you have time to bring your grades up. No TV and no sleepovers until I get a positive progress report from your teachers. Is that understood?"

Donnie: (Disappointed) "Yes Sir."

Father: "Hey, I still love you." (Gives Donnie a hug) "How about we get some ice cream out of the freezer and tell me how you got that A in woodworking. That's a pretty big achievement."

Donnie: "Sure Dad!"

Notice anything different? You should have. There was a big difference between the first father/son conversation and the second. In the first conversation, the father treated the symptom and not the problem. If left at that, the problem will remain. In the second situation, the father identified the problems by asking pointed questions and was able to provide a solution. He addressed the problem, not the symptom.

Are you treating symptoms or problems? Are you wasting valuable resources treating symptoms? Are you taking time to ask the deeper questions to see what the real problem is? Are you taking time to get the basics down pat so when you try to do advanced things (skills, plays, thinking) you will succeed? Are your emotions getting in the way of asking pointed questions and receiving feedback that may indicate that you are part of the problem?

Chapter 3

Leading From the Front

Situation 1, Being a Jumpmaster

Everyone assigned to the Army's 82nd Airborne Division must be "Airborne" qualified and on jump status, which means we all jump out of perfectly good airplanes and hope our parachutes work. The people in charge of airborne operations are known as Jumpmasters and maybe 5% of all the people on jump status are Jumpmasters.

Being a Jumpmaster in the Army is tough. First, you have to go to a special school where the failure rate is 50-60% for an average class. Then once trained, a Jumpmaster has an incredible amount of responsibility. He is responsible for conducting mock training to prepare jumpers for airborne operations; checking jumpers to ensure their equipment is safe for airborne operations; and during the jump, Jumpmasters are responsible for everything inside the aircraft, outside the aircraft, and exiting all jumpers. Every jumpers' life is in the hands of the Jumpmaster and if anything goes wrong, the Jumpmaster is held accountable.

I loved being a Jumpmaster and volunteered to be a Jumpmaster every chance I could. Being a Jumpmaster is a way of life to me even now; so much so, I even wrote a book on the subject. I especially loved being the Primary Jumpmaster, the Jumpmaster overall in charge. My passion for being a Jumpmaster was so high that I voluntarily trained over 20 Jumpmaster students on my own time (all passed Jumpmaster training on their first attempt).

Most Primary Jumpmasters did not give "Prejump," a 5-page list of actions that must be recited by memory to the jumpers by the Jumpmaster, but I always did for two main reasons. First of all, reciting "Prejump" from memory to 60-120 jumpers gave them confidence that I knew what I was doing. Secondly, I was an officer and this was another chance for me to "lead from the front" (many officers pawned off this task to a non-commissioned officer for whatever reason, but that is leading from the rear, in my opinion).

I would always conduct a rehearsal with my Jumpmaster team prior to mock training for the jumpers. This rehearsal ensured the team was on the "same sheet of music" and allowed me the opportunity to validate the competency of my Jumpmaster team. If any retraining needed to be performed, it would be done here. To do so in front of the jumpers would be too late as the jumpers would lose confidence in our ability to execute the airborne operation safely.

At this Jumpmaster rehearsal, I also distributed PowerPoint slide handouts to my team describing how we would conduct our mock training and loading of the aircraft. Why? I know it may seem excessive, but covering the details of how you will work together as a team sets the whole operation up for success. Jumpers get their first impression of their Jumpmaster team during "Prejump" and mock door training. If you don't inspire confidence in the jumpers here, they will not have much confidence in you in the air.

By leading from the front, I inspired others to want to be like me. By leading from the front, jumpers came to me to have their equipment checked. By leading from the front, I inspired confidence in my Jumpmaster team. By leading from the front, our airborne operations were run smoothly, professionally, and safely.

Situation 2, Motivating employees

Platoon training – We had to participate in a Convoy Live Fire eXercise (CLFX) demonstration when I was a platoon leader. A CLFX is where you shoot live ammunition at enemy targets from a vehicle and my platoon was composed of 40 Soldiers. During the train-up for our CLFX and to help motivate my Soldiers, I offered to do 100 push-ups while wearing 25-lb body armor for each scenario done to standard each day. That motivated the Soldiers to work hard for three reasons: one, they weren't sure I could do it at first; two, they could watch their platoon leader do push-ups (something that never happens); and three, this gave the Soldiers bragging rights about their platoon leader. By and far one of the greatest results was that we bonded.

After each After Action Review (AAR)*, my Soldiers saw that I was a man of my word, that I held them to the training standard, and that we were ready to do our wartime mission. Had I not been there leading, watching, evaluating, and providing incentives to perform, we would not have met the standard (which is exactly what happened with the other platoon). And if you are wondering how many push-ups I performed, it was about 1,000.

Leading from the front means that you don't direct others to do something you aren't willing to perform or you haven't performed yourself in the past. Leading from the front means that when training is being conducted, you supervise it. Leading from the front means you stand up for your section/subordinates/family. When things go wrong, you take responsibility. When things go right and you are recognized by superiors or peers, you deflect the praise to your subordinates. Leading from the front always means choosing the hard right over the easy wrong.

*After Action Review (AAR)- An AAR is where one describes his performance- what went right, what went wrong, and what one thinks he can do better in that situation next time. An AAR many times also has a senior leader/observer who watched the event and gives feedback on what he observed, what you should have done, and what you can do better in the future.

Situation 3, Parent apology

"Son, I need to apologize to you for raising my voice at you earlier today. What you did was wrong, but I was also wrong in the way I reacted. Please forgive me. Now, let's talk about what you did."

A parent that admits his mistakes to his child earns the respect of the child which in turn softens the child's heart to listen to instruction. A leader must accept responsibility for his actions in order to inspire others over the long-term.

Situation 4, Coach holding the line

John: "I want to play, Coach!"

Coach: "Then why are you always late to practice John?"

John: "I am the best player on the team. I don't need as much practice as the other guys do."

Coach: "That may be true, but the team needs you to be there at practice. Until you can show up on time to practice, you can sit on the bench."

John: "Well, I quit then!"

In this example, you have a coach leading from the front thinking in the best interest of the team and you have a player who exemplifies selfishness. The coach is responsible for building a team, not an individual. Sometimes it may come at a great loss initially, but the team will overcome. In fact, I had a coach who went through this situation. The selfish player was humbled and later developed into a leader of the team with help from the coach.

Leading from the front requires integrity. You must be a man of your word. Your people must be able to count on you. And to count on you, they must believe in you which leads to my next point. Leading from the front also means your employees/ team/and children trust you. An organization/team/ family that lacks trust will not be productive, but will be counter productive. Sit the people that don't trust each other down, talk through why they don't trust each other, provide a common goal, develop reachable objectives, and check on them regularly to keep on track.

Do you lead by example? Do you know how to do or have you done the tasks required of your people? Do you ask people to do things you wouldn't do yourself? Do you accept responsibility for your actions and your team's actions? When you make a mistake, do you take responsibility for your actions and apologize to those affected by your mistake? When things go well for the organization, do you deflect the praise to your employees/team/children? When things go bad, do you accept responsibility or are you quick to blame others?

Chapter 4

Taking Care of Others

Situation 1, Superior worker

I had this tremendous leader who worked for me. His name was Sergeant (SGT) Tate. SGT Tate was one of the best leaders of Soldiers I have ever come across. He was a squad leader in charge of ten Soldiers. He knew everything about his Soldiers, made sure their pay was "ok", made them take classes to better themselves, disciplined them when needed, and praised them when warranted. He led from the front and he always accomplished every task given him with amazing results. SGT Tate was everyone's "go to" guy.

In fact, I made SGT Tate a Platoon Sergeant over more senior ranking non-commissioned officers. A SGT is never given the position of Platoon Sergeant, but that did not stop me. SGT Tate was the right man for the job and what he didn't know, he made up for in enthusiasm and willingness to learn. For six months, he did an awesome job! Morale was up and our ability to accomplish our missions had never been better.

But there was a problem, SGT Tate was SGT Tate. SGT Tate was so good at getting things done and taking care of other people that his previous leadership failed to send him to the schools he needed to get promoted. SGT Tate was too "valuable" to have gone to any school!

It pained me, but I fired SGT Tate and sent him to school so he could be promoted and assume more leadership positions (When I said I fired him, I gave him no choice but to go to school and I gave him an outstanding evaluation report for the time he served with me). I searched for two months and interviewed about 15-20 people before replacing SGT Tate. Ninety percent of the people I interviewed had the rank and the skills for the job, but in my opinion, they weren't leaders and couldn't lead by example.

Leaders of all levels must take care of their people even if it causes some temporary pain for the organization. The benefit in the long-term far outweighs the pain in the short-term. There are many different ways of taking care of people. Let's look at another situation.

Situation 2, Think about others

It is 4:30 PM and you are finishing up the day's work and looking forward to going home. But before you can get out the door, your boss comes over to you and says, "I need this report/task/or whatever accomplished by first thing tomorrow morning." This isn't a once in awhile occurrence that your boss couldn't control. He does this on a regular basis and, by the way, this task will take you 2-3 hours to perform. So, you are seeing red for the next 20 minutes, stuck at work doing this task, and your wife is mad at you because you missed dinner and can't help with the kids.

Is this taking care of your subordinates? No, this is poor leadership by a boss that doesn't care, doesn't understand, and/or has no concept of time management. A good leader would give the project to the subordinate in advance and allow enough time for completion of the task within the normal work day or an established timeframe. A cut off time for the boss's "good ideas" should be established in this particular case. Every decision a leader makes affects his employees. A leader must think of the big picture and then drill it down to how it affects his organization. Let's look at another situation.

Situation 3, Time off

Boss: "Sally, do you have anything important that has to get done today?"

Sally: "Yes, I have to get the budget report finished."

Boss: "Can John do it?"

Sally: "Well, yes, he can."

Boss: "Good. It is a beautiful day outside and I know how much you wanted to see your son's baseball game today. I want you to take the rest of the day off. I appreciate all you do for us. Now go spend some time with your family and have fun."

Sally: "But."

Boss: "No but's about it! Go. You've earned it."

Note: John must be informed, have the time to accomplish the task, and must be able to accomplish the task to standard. You, the manager, must manage and understand what your employee's abilities and limitations are in order to accomplish objectives, not only today, but also tomorrow and into the future.

Situation 4, Recognizing Peers

While pursuing my MBA, I worked with one study group for two years. At the end of the two years, we had a graduation dinner with the faculty and our class. Prior to the graduation dinner, I created some certificates of appreciation for my group members that I asked the director of the program to sign and allow me to present to my group members at this dinner. He agreed.

During the awards recognition part of the dinner, I called up each group member and said a few great things about each one of them. Once they were all up on center stage, I presented each of them with the awards. My group members were not expecting this at all. How did it make them feel? They felt honored about this recognition in front of their peers and superiors. It was great!

Situation 5, Recognizing Employees

We had to put on a Convoy Live Fire eXercise (CLFX) demonstration when I was a platoon leader. A CLFX is where you shoot live ammunition at enemy targets from a vehicle and my platoon was composed of 40 Soldiers. Now, my platoon was already trained in the CLFX task and we were rehearsing three different scenarios we would be presenting to over 50 key senior leaders the next day. During our rehearsal, my platoon's performance was horrible and embarrassing. It was as if they had forgotten all their training!

I pulled my Platoon Sergeant (second in charge) aside from the troops and told him, "We can rehearse these scenarios one time each if done to standard or until 2 AM in the morning if not. I don't care which, but we are not going to leave this place until we perform to standard!" Forty minutes later all scenarios were performed to standard and we went home. The next day, my Platoon Sergeant and I briefed the key leaders on the different scenarios we would demonstrate and the train-up time required. Then, my Soldiers performed the exercise to perfection.

An hour after the exercise, my Platoon Sergeant and I were told to be at the company in 30 minutes because the Battalion Commander (BC), the CEO of our organization, wanted to speak to us. We were led to believe he was furious, so we wondered what we had done wrong.

Instead of being angry, the BC pinned Army Achievement Medals on the chests of my Platoon Sergeant and me. We later found out, the senior Colonel we briefed said it was the best presentation he had ever seen from someone of my rank. Well, my Platoon Sergeant and I could have left it at that and patted ourselves on the back for a job well done. But we were not solely responsible for the successful presentation. I convinced my BC to recognize five of my Soldiers with Army Achievement Medals and I got the Colonel (a Group Commander- i.e. a higher organization CEO) to recognize every one of my Soldiers with a Group coin and a Certificate of

Achievement. A true leader does not take credit for himself, but instead recognizes and promotes his employees for their roles in the success of the organization.

Situation 6, Checking on the basics

When my father was in the Army, he served in many levels of command and retired as a Lieutenant General. In each leadership position he held, he would check on the troops in the field and at their installations on a regular basis. My dad would make a point to do three things on every visit to an installation which were: Point 1, Check the sanitary conditions to include the restrooms; Point 2, Check on the operations; and Point 3, Talk openly and candidly with the troops (workers). We will discuss points 1 and 2 here and develop point 3 in Chapter 14, Counsel of 2 or 3.

Why would my father check on sanitary conditions to include the restrooms? Think about it. If the restrooms are nasty, are leaders taking care of people? Absolutely not! This is a great indicator that leaders are neglecting other areas also. Unsanitary conditions equal sick people which translates into low productivity. We owe our people and our organization decent working conditions. It is the responsibility of the leader to ensure that proper resources are in place, the resources are being taken care of, and the resources are being used properly.

Once we know the basics are being done right, we can focus on the operations. Checking on the operations is taking care of people because we need to know the conditions people are working in and the standards being enforced. We also need to know if the leaders understand their role (the mission they are responsible for in meeting the organization's goal) and if they understand the organization goal. If the operations are not synched and being done to standard, then our organization will fail in its mission and that is not taking care of people.

Situation 7, Family Time

> Dad: "John, Jeff, Melissa, Zach come sit down. We are getting ready to plan some family days for the summer. What are some things each one of you wants to do and who do you want to do it with or bring along?"

Your family is important. You need to find out what they want to do and not always do what you want to do. And some of your family members will just want some alone time with you and others may want everyone around. Listen to their needs, understand how to speak to them, and accommodate what you can within limits.

Situation 8, Discipline

> Child: "But dad, all the other kids are allowed to do that!"

> Dad: "What their parents allow is their parents business. That is unacceptable behavior in my book, because it is disrespectful."

> Child: "But dad!"

> Dad: "I said, "No."

> Child: "That's not fair. I hate you."

> Dad: "I am sorry you feel that way. Furthermore, what you just said is mean and while my decision may seem unfair in your eyes, my decision is final. My job is to be your parent, not your friend."

Taking care of people means disciplining as needed and conducting preventive discipline. Disciplining is not an easy task, nor a fun task, but it must be done.

Situation 9, Practice

Player: "Coach, why do we always have to do grass drills? Can't we take a break?"

Coach: "Do you want to be winners or losers?"

Player: "Winners."

Coach: "Then we need to be the best conditioned team. Now, get those legs up!"

Player: "But we are tired!"

Coach: "Tired? You don't know the meaning of the word yet and that remark will cost you an extra 50. Hit it!"

An out of shape team is a losing team. Taking care of your players' means getting them in shape and getting them in shape also helps to prevent injuries.

Situation 10, Teaching

Daughter: "Dad, I hate math! Why do I have to learn it? I will never use Algebra!"

Dad: "Sweetie, everything we have and use are based on math principles from the house we live in to the roads we drive on."

Daughter: "Come on Dad! Who cares?"

Dad: "Ok, let's stop the complaining, calm down, and we will go through this problem step-by-step. No yelling or screaming. Alright?"

Daughter: "But Dad!"

Dad: Now a little firmer, "Alright?"

Daughter: "Ok."

Dad: "Ok, step 1, let's identify the problem…."

Daughter: At the end of the homework thirty minutes later, "This is so easy Dad."

Dad: "Well, maybe. But it was very hard until we learned when and how to ask the right questions."

Taking care of others means teaching them lessons even when they don't want to learn. It is your job as a leader to prepare the people you are responsible for to operate successfully in your absence.

Situation 11, Self-sacrifice

On Christmas Day in 2004, three captains pulled guard duty in Fallujah, Iraq. Two of those captains were the primary staff (senior advisors) to a Brigade Commander (CEO) and were exempt from ever pulling duty. Two lieutenants (lower in rank to the captains) also pulled duty. So, five out of over 300 eligible officers on the base volunteered to pull guard duty so that Soldiers could enjoy the day off and partake of the feast prepared for them. That is taking care of people. That is leadership in action.

It has been said that, "no one cares how much you know, until you show how much you care." Think about it. Taking care of others covers the full spectrum of rewarding good performance, thinking about how your decisions affect others, discipline, and being there for your subordinates/ teammates/and children.

When was the last time you gave someone time off? When was the last time you recognized an employee? When was the last time you took your family's feelings into consideration? When was the last time you performed preventive discipline? When was the last time you put others first before yourself?

Chapter 5

Counseling

Situation 1, Evaluation report time

> Manager: "Hey John, come into my office."

> Employee: "Yes, Sir."

> Manager: "John, here is your annual evaluation. Just sign on the bottom line. Any questions?"

> Employee: (Confused) "No."

> Manager: "I am glad we had this talk John. Keep up the good work."

Situation 2, Negative performance counseling

> Manager: "John, this work is pathetic! Get your act together or find a new job. Don't let me have to tell you this again."

Do any of these situations seem familiar? These situations represent what most people understand as counseling. There is a third situation and that is no counseling whatsoever. "Who has time for counseling?" is the excuse.

I have come to learn that most people view counseling as a negative event. The reason: Leaders do not know how to counsel properly. Counseling should not be dreaded. It should be an event both the counselor and the counselee look forward too! Counseling is one of the greatest tools to develop future leaders.

But I don't have time to counsel, you say. Actually, you have it all wrong. You don't have time not to counsel!

Counseling sets the standard for your employees and your loved ones to follow. If people do not know the standards, how can they reach the goal? If you don't sit down and talk to your employees and family members, how will you learn what motivates them and what is going on in their lives?

There are two types of counseling. Formal and informal. Formal counseling should be scheduled at least quarterly, while informal counseling can, and should, happen on a near daily basis.

Formal counseling consists of a written record where you write down the non-negotiable standards and develop reasonable goals for employees to achieve in a specified time period. At the end of the rating period, you compare the performance to the agreed upon goals. If he has exceeded the goals, reward the employee and create more challenging goals. If the goals have not been achieved, you need to know why and possibly conduct retraining on deficient skills.

During the first formal counseling session, I like to let the employee know my background, who I am, and what I expect. I have a handout with that same information that I give to the employee for future reference. I then give the employee my full, undivided attention and ask the employee about himself and his background. Once I know a little bit about the employee, I ask him what he thinks his responsibilities and duties are and then we set our goals and objectives. Sometimes the employee's goals may not be as high as yours, but if yours are realistic, stick to your guns and make the employee raise his standards.

If you have an evaluation report format that your organization uses, fill it out in pencil the way you would rate that person today (for sessions after the initial counseling, fill out comments in addition to ratings). Explain that your assessment will be adjusted in future counseling sessions based on performance (this is why it is filled out in pencil if you haven't figured that out already). There are two benefits associated with the pencil technique: one, the employee knows where he stands at all times so there are no surprises at evaluation time and two, when it comes time to prepare the evaluation for turn-in, you already have all the achievements documented.

Let's now talk about informal counseling. A leader must know and inspire his people. He does this through daily interaction. He not only asks them about their personal lives, but also about how they are coming along with the tasks assigned. Asking how they are coming along prevents unwelcome surprises (failures) later when the tasks are due. By asking where they are at and what problems they are experiencing, you can keep abreast of the situation, adjust the task due date if warranted, and/or train and resource the person as needed to accomplish the mission. I call this setting each other up for success. You set your subordinate up for success which in turn sets you up for success. We will talk more about setting up others for success in Chapter 25.

Counseling is taking care of people. Recognizing someone for doing something right and pulling aside someone to correct what is wrong creates a positive work environment where standards are enforced. But don't be all business. Your employees need to know that you care about them and what matters to them. This builds true loyalty, improves performance, and makes everyone's life richer.

Situation 3, Counseling with children

I had the awesome privilege of going to the White House lawn and seeing the President of the United States land in Marine One. I was able to bring along my best friend, my mother, my 10-year old daughter, and two of my daughter's friends. We arrived about two-and-a-half-hours early so we could do some sight-seeing while waiting. My daughter's two friends were friends with her, but not friends with each other.

After we parked our car and began walking, Julia called her mother on a cell phone and was complaining about not having a good time (keep in mind that not more than 10 minutes had passed). After 5 minutes of listening to this, my best friend got that nightmare look on his face that this was going to be a long day. I sat the other two girls down and told them to stay put. I saw that Julia had handed the phone to my mother.

I motioned for my mother to hand the phone to me and I listened to Julia's mom for a moment. I then said that the problem lies with all the girls, that they were all at fault, and that I would fix it. She wasn't sure, but I reassured her that I had the situation under control and for her not to give in to her daughter. I then gave the phone to Julia and she talked to her mom for another couple of minutes. After Julia finished, I took the phone from her and gave it to my mother and told my mother, "Do not give this phone back to Julia. There will be no more phone calls."

I then sat the three girls together with Julia sitting in the middle and began a short counseling session. "Girls, I am going to talk and you are going to listen until I am finished. Understand? Good. What happened earlier today is ancient history. Olivia and Kathleen, you need to know what Julia is going through. Her Nana is very sick and may die, just imagine if that was your mom or grandma getting ready to die how you would feel? And Julia, your mommy is going through a tough time. She does not need any more phone calls to make her worry even more. She has enough on her plate. Now Julia, if you don't want to feel left out, then you can't just sit there all quiet. You have to participate also, Ok? Good. Alright girls, listen up. We have the chance to see the President of the United States today. Do you know how many people get that opportunity? Not many. This is a special event and we are going to have fun. I will not put up with any more of this negative behavior. From now on, I want you all to walk in a line of three so no one feels left out. Ready to go? Yes, Kathleen."

"But dad, we tried to involve Julia."

"Kathleen the past is over. Everyone will be a team. Ok! Let's get moving."

We started walking. Every couple of minutes, I would have to remind them to stay three in a line as one would lag behind. I also started asking one girl a question, listened to the answer, and then asked the other two girls the same question. When they finished, I would ask another question and have a different girl answer first. After about ten minutes of this, I stated, "When we can all say we are happy, then I will buy you ice cream."

As we came to a nice park, I mentioned, "Do you want to have lunch here?" All the girls said, "Yes." So, I told them to all agree on a tree for us to sit under. We sat down and then I made some jokes about myself and then began asking questions like, "So what was your most embarrassing moment in school? What is your favorite amusement park ride and why?" and other open ended questions with the same pattern of calling on a different girl first. Within minutes they were all intently listening to one another's answers and laughing. I then asked them to create a little skit and perform for us, which they did, and then we had to rush to the White House to be on time.

So, what happened at the end of the day? Two new friends were created and we all had a great time. In this particular case of counseling, the girls needed someone to guide them in the process. Left to fend for themselves, one child would have felt left out for sure. Instead, I used the positive reinforcement of the ice cream (which we got twice since they were so good and it was so hot outside) and guided them as they slipped into potential trouble until I wasn't needed anymore.

As a leader, you have to make the judgment of how much involvement is required for each subordinate. For those that lack maturity and don't have any or many skills, you tell them what to do and watch over them. For those that are more mature and have some skills, you give some guidelines and interject as needed. For those that are mature and have a lot of skills, you guide and encourage them so they find their own solution. These thoughts are developed more using both positive and negative situations in Chapter 12, Developing Others.

Do you take time to counsel your teammates/employees/ children? When you do take time, are you just correcting bad behavior and yelling at them? Do you conduct any positive counseling? Are you trying to develop your teammates/ employees/children? Are you learning what motivates them? Do you really care about your players/employees/children?

Tip: When counseling, always end on a positive note. People need hope and you want to inspire the person to improve.

Chapter 6

Discipline

Situation 1, Insulting threats

Have you ever heard, "What the h*** are you doing? You need to get your head out of your a** and get with it!" or "If you do that again, you're FIRED!" or "Get out of my sight! Since you can't do the job right, I'm going to do it myself." Oh, and by the way, this is happening in front of your peers or subordinates.

Is this a productive way to solve a problem or correct a mistake? No! This will only put the person being yelled at on the defensive and shut down any possibility of solving the problem or problem behavior. Too often, we confuse punishment with discipline and there is a big difference between discipline and punishment. More on that in a minute.

Situation 2, Excessive discipline

One of your basketball players blows his defensive coverage and the opponent scores a basket. You react by pulling him out and making him do 50 push-ups in front of the rest of the team and the crowd attending the game.

Is the correction appropriate for the mistake and is the correction being given at the proper location? I think you know the answer is no on both accounts.

Now, let's discuss the difference between discipline and punishment. Discipline is used to correct negative behavior. Punishment is you did something wrong, you got caught, and now you must pay the price. A good leader will discipline his workers when needed and not punish them. Punishment only builds resentment while discipline can be a tool to correct the problem behavior. When one administers discipline, however, one must do it in a firm but caring way. If you don't show that you care, you are wasting your time correcting the behavior and the discipline will be interpreted as punishment instead.

An example of disciplining my daughter follows. When my daughter does something wrong, I don't raise my voice and yell angrily at her. Instead, I make sure I am calm and then call her over. I have her tell me what she did that was wrong (if she doesn't know or hesitates, I prompt her). I then calmly and firmly tell her why it was wrong and, that because I love her, I am not going to tolerate that behavior. I then discuss our method to correct the behavior (paddle, restriction, redoing the task, etc.)*. Finally, after administering the discipline, I hug my daughter and tell her I love her. The problem is then over and we go about our business as if nothing had happened. Two key points to remember are never discipline when angry and you should not enjoy administering the discipline.

* Discipline. The type of discipline will change with the age and maturity of the individual. A young child may need to be paddled to prevent a negative behavior from reoccurring, but a child ten and older would probably do better with restriction along with correctional training/ extra duties (Paddling a ten year-old would be punishment). Furthermore, child abuse is never acceptable in any shape or form.

Now, how does one discipline at the office? I have found two effective ways. One is when disciplining the employee, I formally bring the employee in and then give the employee my full, undivided attention and we talk about the problem. I then share the story above about my daughter or a similar event and insert some humor into the discipline process to help put the employee at ease. This method is effective when one has a normally hard charging employee that has now started to make some bad decisions.

The other effective way is to remain firm with the employee the whole time, but let the employee know up front and at the end that you care about him and that this behavior must be corrected. The second method is generally used when the employee has consistently been a poor performer.

Let's talk a little more in depth about discipline. First off, the discipline must match the infraction. For example, if a Soldier doesn't show up for duty, take his time from him. If your child doesn't clean his room, have him clean the house. If your star player doesn't show up for practice, bench him. If an employee doesn't type a critical document correctly, show the employee the standard and have him retype it to the standard.

The discipline should tie in with the type of behavior you want to correct. Secondly, the discipline needs to be weighted to the infraction incurred. If you discipline too harshly, it will build resentment. If you discipline too light, it will not deter the behavior. The level of discipline is also determined by the individual you are disciplining. If this is a repeat offender, the discipline should be more severe. If it is a first offense, out of character, and the individual is sorry (not for being caught, but for the action committed), then the discipline should be less severe.

Discipline on a sports team poses special challenges, however, as all players must be treated equally or there will be a break down in cohesion and the team will suffer.

For example, if the star player gets away with everything while the bench warmer is punished, this will breed animosity and reinforce the out-of-control behavior of the star player.

Disciplining the team as a whole with conditioning drills for lack of motivation, going-through-the-motion performance, foul mouths, tardiness, and unsportsmanlike conduct on and off the field are great motivators for players to shape up physically, mentally, and morally.

A final word about discipline. Every good leader will take the time to develop an employee/teammate/or child. Discipline reinforces where the boundaries are, shows true caring, and develops tomorrow's leaders. A lack of discipline will lower the standards; lead to chaos; and create selfish, irresponsible leaders.

Take a hard look at yourself. Do you discipline or punish your employees/players/children? Does your discipline fit the offense committed? Do you have a set of standards in place your organization abides by? Do your people, peers, and/or children know that you care? Does your discipline develop others? If you were in their shoes, how would you want to be treated?

Also, do you want to be yelled at? Think of how you react to being yelled at. Ninety percent of the time you tune out the person yelling and get angry yourself. No one likes to be yelled at! It is one thing to yell at someone if it will save their life or prevent bodily harm, but a constant yeller is another thing altogether. When disciplining you may need to raise your voice to show emphasis at times, but there is no need to yell most of the time. Remember, discipline is used to change negative behavior, not reinforce it. After the discipline has been administered, act as if the incident never happened.

Chapter 7

Do as I Say, Not as I Do (Practice What You Preach)

Situation 1, Company leadership

A friend of mine works for a company that is going through a financial crisis and the leaders recognize that there is a need for change. The leaders are stressing the need to realign the company, to cut costs, to work smarter, and that leadership must set the example. But, the president is having an affair with one of the employees, the Chief Financial Officer (CFO) is leaving work everyday by 4 PM, and the company executives work in this beautiful office while the majority of employees work in hot cubicles or worse conditions. What kind of signal does this send? Not the one leadership intends.

Situation 2, Fatherly example

A father tells his son to study hard and not to cheat, but then the father cheats on his income taxes and brags about it to anyone who will listen. What signal does that send to the son?

"Do as I say, not as I do" is a recipe for failure that builds resentment in an organization or a home. A leader must walk the talk. Even if the leader is walking the talk, but the employees perceive he is not, then the leader is not walking the talk. Perception is reality. Let me say that again for emphasis. Perception is reality. Their perception, not yours, equals reality for those around you.

For example, in the first situation above where we have the CFO leaving at 4 PM, maybe the CFO comes in at 6 AM and has to pick up her kids from school because she is a single parent. If the employees don't know these facts, then they perceive that either the CFO is not committed to change or the

CFO is getting preferential treatment. They may even perceive that management is "sticking it to the employees again and they want me to work harder, yeah, right!" Perception, even if wrong, is reality.

In the second situation, kids learn who they are going to be from their parents. The example they perceive we are setting will guide their rebellion/acceptance of authority. If a child cheats, gets caught, and you discipline him, how is that going to make him feel? He is going to lash out at you, because you are a hypocrite.

Is everyone a hypocrite in some way? Yes. The trick is when you find out that you are or have been hypocritical, admit to your failure, correct it, and move forward. Take a deep look at yourself; do you see any areas that need to improve? Are you a practicing hypocrite? What signals are you sending to your subordinates/teammates/children? Now ask others that know you for feedback. Remember, don't shoot the messenger! Their perception is reality.

Situation 3, Night before a big game

Coach: "I want everyone in bed, alone, and asleep by 10 PM tonight. There will be no drinking of alcohol at all. I want everyone rested. We will meet Saturday morning in the gym at 8 AM so all of you can get your minds' focused for the game."

Now, if the kids see the coach having a beer or two, how are they going to feel? Upset of course! Upset so much that the "screw him" and "if he can do it, I can do it" mentality sets in. We have to practice what we preach or the opposite effect will happen; guaranteed.

Situation 4, Sex

I am a Christian and in the Bible it tells us not to have sex before marriage. I also want to impart this belief on my eleven year-old daughter. Now, I am a single, dating parent who regrettably divorced many years ago.

If I tell my daughter to wait to have sex until she is married and she sees me dating women and having sex before marriage, is she going to listen to me? No, of course not! I have to set the example in my own dating life and I tell you it is tough, but you have to practice what you preach.

I am now engaged to a wonderful woman and I am really looking forward to getting married. Because my fiancé and I are waiting to make love until we get married, does that send a strong signal to my daughter? You bet!

Are you holding your employees/players/family to a higher standard than yourself? Look at yourself professionally and morally. Are you being a hypocrite in your own eyes? What about their eyes? Remember, their perception is reality, not yours. So are you practicing what you preach? If not, begin today. No one is perfect, but when you fall, confess it and turn away from it. Then, get back on the horse again and practice what you preach. Your family/peers/superiors/and team must trust you.

Chapter 8

Setting the Standards

Situation 1, Raising the standard

My first duty assignment as an officer in the military was in the 82nd Airborne Division. Within the first week of arriving at my unit, a company (organization) of 120 Soldiers, I needed to take a physical fitness test. The Army physical fitness (PT) test is composed of push-ups, sit-ups, and a 2 mile run. Our First Sergeant (1SG) was in charge of the PT test. I spoke to him beforehand and mentioned that I wanted to challenge the Soldiers. He thought it was a good idea. So, on the morning of the test, the 1SG turned over the formation to me so I could address the 70 or so people taking the test that day.

"For those of you that do not know me, my name is Lieutenant Kind, and to make the PT test a little more challenging I am going to make a bet with you. I will do 100 push-ups for any Soldier that can perform more push-ups, sit-ups, or run the 2 miles faster than me. How does that sound?" A loud roar of approval followed and then I turned the formation over to the 1SG. Now, I had no idea how many Soldiers could perform better than me in any of those events, but I was in pretty good shape and didn't think there were too many. My goal was to inspire the Soldiers.

As we took the PT test, no one beat me in push-ups or sit-ups (I did 120+ of each in 2 minutes), but then came the run. One Soldier beat me by about 20 seconds and another beat me by about a second.

As soon as we formed back up, I had the 1SG turn the formation back over to me. I then ordered the Soldiers to gather around me so that everyone had a good view and said, "Looks like I owe y'all 200 push-ups. I will knock out 100 here and

49

another 100 a little while later." Everyone was shocked. They didn't expect me to stay true to my word and as I started knocking out my push-ups, their astonishment was turned to cheering and counting.

After the first 100 push-ups were performed, the 1SG marched us back to the company, turned the company over to me, and then I performed my final 100 push-ups to the cheer of the Soldiers. They were amazed when I did the first 100, but no one believed I would ever do the second 100. They figured I would "let it slide."

What happened here? Yes, this was leading from the front (See Chapter 3), but it was also something even more important. I had raised the standard of expectations. The Soldiers, many of which who would work for me directly in a few weeks, learned that the bare minimum performance would not be acceptable. The bar had been raised. The Soldiers also learned that I was a man of my word.

What if I had shown up in poor shape? What if I hadn't lived up to my promises? A new, lower standard would have been set.

Note: A little education about the differences between officers and non-commissioned officers (NCOs). Officers are like top level executives, they are responsible for the overall organization and for the short and long range planning. Non-commissioned officers, on the other hand, are like front line management as they are in charge of the day-to-day operations. First Sergeants (1SG) and Platoon Sergeants (PSG) are NCOs that are in middle management and responsible for ensuring the front line managers are doing their jobs.

Situation 2, Enforcing the standard

After we had finished the first day of our Convoy Live Fire eXercise (CLFX) training, I instructed my PSG (2nd in charge) and my squad leaders (1st line supervisors) to clean out all the spent brass ammunition casings from our weapons that were left in the vehicles from the CLFX. A CLFX is where you shoot live ammunition at enemy targets from a vehicle. I had them restate to me that there would be no brass left in the vehicles. This would be no small task as the beds of the vehicles were covered (hardened) with sand bags, so there were many nooks and crannies for brass to fall in. Once I was sure they knew the mission, I went back to the headquarters to do paperwork, review that day's training, and adjust the next day's training based on today's performance.

Two hours later I received the call that they were ready for my inspection. I asked if the PSG had inspected and they replied, "Yes." I asked if they were 100% sure I would find no brass and ammo and they replied that I wouldn't. I then stated, "You may dismiss the Soldiers, but I want all leaders to remain and walk through the inspection with me."

As we started the inspection, I lifted a sandbag and found a few brass casings. Then, I found a few more casings under another sandbag. I decided to check a cab and lifted a seat up and found another casing. I looked at my leaders and said this is unacceptable and it needed to be fixed now. I got a dejected, "Yes, Sir" and then one of the squad leaders started to run to the office. I asked him where he was going and he looked at me like I was stupid and responded, "To call the troops and get them back here to clean up the vehicles, Sir!" I responded, "Stop! Get back over here."

I then addressed my leaders, "You, not the Soldiers, will clean these vehicles. You knew the standard and did not uphold it. You will not punish the Soldiers for your mistake. You will stay here and clean for as long as it takes until I find no brass in any vehicle. When you are ready for me to inspect, call me at the office."

My squad leaders were mad at me, mad at themselves, and mad that I was taking away their Friday night! About two more hours and a few hundred more casings later, my leaders called me and I inspected. They met the standard and I released them. Do you think they met the standard the first time on Saturday night? You bet!

There are many leadership principles to learn from here. I defined what standard I would accept that Friday. I had only been the Platoon Leader for two weeks before this exercise and my leaders tested me to see where their left and right limits were just like every subordinate, child, and team does. Not only did I set the standard, but I forced my leaders to do their job. They felt they were "too senior" to pick up casings, but since they failed to supervise and inspect their Soldiers, I deemed it their responsibility to fix the problem. In the future, I never had a problem like this again. My leaders knew if they failed in their responsibilities, I would hold them accountable, not their subordinates.

Situation 3, Free throws

After team practice is over, each player is required to make ten free throws in a row without any misses before being allowed to go home. Whether it takes one try or a thousand; ten free throws in a row is the standard. The minute the coach lets someone get by with nine shots in a row, a new, lower standard is set.

Situation 4, HOV ticket

I was driving on I-66 West leaving Washington, D.C. at 10 minutes before 3 PM. At 3 PM on weekdays, I-66 becomes an HOV (High Occupancy Vehicle) road. My exit was in three miles so I thought, "No problem." Well, there was an accident and I did not get to my exit until 3:04 PM. Guess what? I got pulled over and given a $120 ticket! The officer didn't care what I had to say. Was I mad? You bet! But have I gotten on I-66 again near 3 PM with just me in the vehicle? The answer is most definitely "No!" While a warning ticket or lecture would have sufficed for me, the important thing is a police officer was enforcing a standard.

Situation 5, New job

> You as the new leader: "Do we have a standard operating procedure (SOP) we follow?"
>
> Employee: "We have an SOP, but it hasn't been updated in years so we really don't use it."

As you look through the SOP, you notice that most of the information is outdated or irrelevant and it is no wonder no one follows the SOP any more, but instead creates their own rules. As you continue to read, however, you also see that some key procedures that need to be performed are not being performed either.

This is exactly what I walked into on one job. Within a month, we created a new SOP that transformed our unit from the least respected to the gold standard of our organization because we implemented policies and procedures that were relevant, customer oriented, and customer friendly. We also sold our idea to the CEO and got his top down support behind us which was the key to our success.

Situation 6, Family chores

> Daughter: "I want to go over to Lisa's house and play."
>
> Dad: "Have you done your chores?"
>
> Daughter: "I cleaned my room, but I didn't clean the bathroom because I didn't have any cleanser."
>
> Dad: "Look under the kitchen sink for some cleanser and when you are done you can play."

Remember, before your children can perform their chores, they need to know how to do them. Once you have taught them and given them the appropriate resources so they can do their chores, you have to hold them to the standard. It is easy to not enforce, but when we don't, it makes it that much harder the next time to enforce the standard.

Are you meeting the standards you hold your employees/players/and family to? Are you raising standards that are too low, outdated, or morally/ethically wrong? Are the standards and outcomes easily measured? Are the standards relevant?

Chapter 9

Rights vs. Responsibility

Situation 1, My rights.

"I want my rights!" or "I know my rights!" or "That's not fair!" Ever heard any of these before? Probably said it a few times yourself too, huh? I know I have, but it is the wrong way to do business.

Situation 2, False accusations vs. responsibility

"He was racist. I didn't get the job because I was black, white, yellow, male, female, etc." In a small amount of cases this may be true, but let's look at the real situation most of the time. Why would a manager want to hire a person to work with customers when a person talks like a bum, dresses unprofessionally, and/or shows no professional courtesy? He wouldn't. That isn't racism. That is business sense. The manager has a responsibility to the customers.

Situation 3, Free speech vs. responsibility

"I have the right to say what I want!" You hear it all the time. You don't have the right to yell, "Fire!" or "Bomb!" when there isn't one. Yes, you have the right to say what you want within reason, but you have a responsibility to others to speak productively.

Situation 4, Complaining vs. responsibility

"I have the right to complain." Sure you do, but more importantly you have the responsibility to offer a solution, otherwise you are part of the problem; and an annoying part of the problem at that!

Situation 5, Respect

A young man says, "I deserve respect!" No, no one deserves respect. Respect is earned by being responsible, doing what is right, and excelling at what you do. Respect is also easily lost, but that is another topic.

Note: I am not saying do not respect authority or your elders here. What I am saying is the person demanding respect is usually younger and has not proved himself worthy of respect yet.

Situation 6, Eating vs. responsibility

You have the right to eat food. However, you have the responsibility to earn money to pay for the food you eat.

Situation 7, Discrimination vs. responsibility

You have the right to not be discriminated against, but you have the responsibility to overcome it if you have been discriminated against and you have the responsibility to prevent it from happening to others within the limits of your control.

Situation 8, Possessions vs. responsibility

You have the right to have nice things, but you have the responsibility to earn them legally.

Situation 9, Sex vs. responsibility

"I have the right to sleep with whomever I want." Well, that is debatable and I disagree. However, if you do sleep with whomever and create a child, you have a responsibility to provide for that child.

What am I getting at here? The Constitution gives us all certain rights. Just because you have the right to do something doesn't make the act of doing it right. You have to take responsibility for your actions. If you make a mistake, own up to it. If you enjoy the rights of freedom, then you have the responsibility to fight for freedom and/or support those that do. If you want something, earn it. You have the right to fail, but you have the responsibility to fix your failures.

What does this mean to me as a leader? All eyes are on you at all times. You have a responsibility to your family, team, and organization to do the right thing. When you start focusing on your responsibilities instead of your rights, you have taken a monumental step forward to becoming a true leader. Is it always easy? Absolutely not! One of the hardest decisions I ever made was to give up a career I truly loved so I could raise my daughter. I had the right to stay in that career field, but I had the responsibility as a parent to raise my child.

As a leader, you have the responsibility to look out for the best interests of the whole organization and your section of that organization. That means the people working for you are your family and you must take care of them.

As a parent and a spouse, it means you provide for your family's needs before you buy yourself that new set of golf clubs.

As a coach, it means parents have entrusted you to train their children and push their children, but not to cross the line. You have the responsibility to teach teamwork, to provide discipline, and to build self-confidence.

Situation 10, Responsibility for actions

Dad: "How was lacrosse camp today?"

Daughter: Crying, "Daddy, it was horrible. The coach told me to play attack wing, but my teammates said I was supposed to play D wing. Then everyone said it was my fault because we lost."

Dad: "I am sorry dear. It doesn't feel good, does it?"

Daughter: "No." (Pause) "Daddy?"

Dad: "Yes Sweetie."

Daughter: "Now I know how it feels to be blamed for other people's mistakes. You were right, you have to take responsibility for your own actions and not blame others for your mistakes. I realize I have done this to you and to other kids in school. I don't want to be like that."

Dad: "Kathleen, I am very proud of you. I know it hurts, but you have learned a great lesson that will help you to be a better person. And you know what?"

Daughter: "What?"

Dad: "Tomorrow is a new day, you will do your best, and you and your teammates will have fun."

And so they did, but more importantly here was a ten year-old girl recognizing that you have to take responsibility for your own actions and when you don't, you hurt other people. How proud I was that day!

So, are you more concerned about your rights or responsibilities? What are your responsibilities to your family, team, organization, and country? Are you fulfilling your responsibilities? If not, why?

Chapter 10

Racism, Sexism, Etc.

There is no story to start this chapter as I want to give you the bottom line up front. Racism and sexism have no place in the workplace, sports, or in your personal life. It is unacceptable to discriminate against someone because of race, creed, or sex and it is also unacceptable as an individual to play the "racist/sexist" card. Let me be clear on this. The "racist/sexist" card is when you falsely accuse someone of discriminating against you because you did not get what you wanted. The "racist/sexist" card is not a legitimate complaint when you have failed to perform. The "racist/sexist" card is also when you use your race/sex as a weapon for unearned advancement.

We all have biases and personal preferences. You as a leader need to pick the best person for the job, period. Whether you are white, black, yellow, male, or female; there is one standard. Set it, then enforce it. This is so important it bears restating. Set the standard and then enforce it.

Most people have been discriminated against at some point in their life. I have been discriminated against many times for many different reasons. What measures who I am is how I reacted to those situations. I could have accepted that behavior, but I didn't. I could have retaliated, but I didn't. I chose to work harder, overcome, and when put in leadership positions, not allow that type of behavior to take place. I took responsibility for my actions.

When you come on board as a leader, you need to inform all your subordinates that racism/sexism will not be tolerated and everyone will be treated the same and adhere to this one standard. Then, you must enforce the standard.

My leadership experience has taught me that eighty percent of the complaints of racism, sexism, etc. have come from an individual that uses this excuse as a crutch to get what he/she wants or get out of doing something he/she does not want to do. The "racist/sexist" card places fear into a lot of people. If you as a leader set the example and run an organization that does not tolerate racism/sexism, it will be evident if you have an unjustified complaint.

For example, when I was Captain of the Ranger Challenge team* (a varsity sport for military ROTC**), I was accused by a cadet of being racist. She felt I kicked her off the team because she was female and black. I was shocked to say the least, but it turns out I didn't even have to defend myself. My other cadets, black and white males and one female, came to my defense. My superiors didn't believe the false allegation either. Why? I had set the standards and everyone knew my character. The cadet in question didn't show up for practice, so she didn't deserve to be on the team. Color or race never entered into the equation, but she didn't get her way, so she tried to save face by playing the "racist/sexist" card.

Note: I said in my experience, 80% of the racism/sexism cases were unfounded. That means 20% of complaints were legitimate. I squashed the bug in my organizations when and wherever I saw it. Most of the time, with a little education, the behavior was corrected because the accused didn't know or believe that what he/she was doing was offensive and wrong. Racism/sexism can be against any sex or color and is never appropriate or acceptable in any form.

*Ranger Challenge consists of constructing a one man rope bridge over water and crossing it, a 12 mile forced march with weapon and back pack weighing 35 lbs, weapons assembly/disassembly, land navigation, a Physical Fitness test, and a written test. The events are conducted over a two day time period. A team is made up of nine members and the top eight scores count.

**ROTC- Reserve Officer Training Corps. A program offered at most colleges and universities for students aspiring to learn leadership and/or become officers in the military.

Situation 1, Counseling of females in an open place.

I make it a practice to never counsel females privately in my office. I always counsel in an open area where other people can see us. Why? It is for the safety of both of us as it leaves no room for questions of harassment or inappropriate touching. If I am counseling on a personal or disciplinary issue, I have a trusted subordinate of mine (usually my number 2) present.

Some of you may think this practice is a double-standard and you are entitled to your opinion. I see this as setting up all people involved for success and preventing even the perception of sexual harassment from emerging.

Are you racist? Do you discriminate against people of another color or sex? If an outsider looked in at your organization/home/team, what would he see? Do you encourage diversity? Do you evaluate people differently because of color/gender/weight/or beauty?

Situation 2, MBA group diversity

My Master in Business Administration (MBA) study group was made up of five people: Srini, a brown man originally from India who is a computer expert, math genius, and very creative; Derril, a Southern black man who is a computer expert, creative, and always willing to help others; Carla, a Hispanic woman with tremendous writing ability and organizational skills; Brenda, a white woman with great writing skills and business sense; and me, a white guy with a military background, presentation skills, and a sense for practicality. We were a very diverse group with completely different backgrounds. Each one of us brought certain strengths to the group.

In completing each of our group projects and presentations, one of us would take the lead and then get input from the others. It never ceased to amaze me how awesome our final product would always be. And do you know why our products were awesome? It was because of the different thinking processes we had, our different backgrounds, and when combined together, we looked at a problem almost every way imaginable. Our diversity was our strength. When one person said one thing, it always triggered a thought in someone else's head. Our group product was always better than any one of our individual efforts because of the counsel of others and our diversity.

Situation 3, Team integration

How many times have you seen a team where the white people hang out with the white people and the black people hang out with the black people? Is this an integrated team? No!

A team that is separated by color off the field will never be the best it can be on the field. The coach must step up and integrate the team. On road trips, it might be assigning black and white players to sit with one another. In training, it might be assigning work details to integrated teams of two to five players. The coach must also talk to his players and treat his players fairly (no favoritism in skin color, in jobs assigned, discipline, or rewards). As the players integrate, they will become a team; friendships will bloom, and racism will decrease.

Note: Some players will not like each other. Disliking someone for how they act is one thing, disliking them because of their color/sex and not getting to know them is quite another. Racism/sexism is sustained by ignorance.

Situation 4, Wedding

When I turned sixteen, my parents and I went to a wedding in North Carolina. The parents of the groom were and are best friends of my parents along with being like second parents to me.

As we drove to the wedding, the only thoughts on my mind were that I was happy for the bride and groom getting married and the fact that I wanted to get my driver's license.

Now, my parents and I traveled from Georgia and arrived at the family mixer which was being held at a hotel because there were over 400 people attending the wedding. Once we walked in, it seemed like everything stopped and you could hear a pin drop. Everyone was staring at us like we were in the wrong place until the hosts greeted us warmly. It was very evident that many people did not want us there, a few others were indifferent, and a small few (those that knew us) were downright happy to see us. What was all the fuss? We were the only white people there!

For the first time in my life, I truly understood what a person feels like when they don't initially "fit in" because of skin color. You could cut the tension with a knife at first (at least I thought so). It is one thing to be disliked because your personalities don't get along, but skin color is another thing. But as we got to know people and they got know us, we just became part of the family. Did some still not like us because we were white, sure, but I figured that was their problem, not mine.

Do you have someone you work with from a different background/skin color/sex? Do you think that they have a different perspective to add? Have you taken time to get to know them personally or stayed away emotionally because they are "different?" How do you think they feel if they look different than everyone else at first? A little nervous? Out of place? Experiencing racism?

Set one standard for all. Our nation will be better for it. Whether at home or work or play, the output from the team/organization will vastly improve.

Chapter 11

Know Your Audience

Situation 1, Speak *with* your audience, not above your audience

In developing the USAF budget, the Air Staff works on the POM in the spring, the BES in the summer, submits the PBR to OSD in the fall, gets PBDs and PDMs in the winter while working on the PB, submits the PB in Feb to Congress and then the PPBE cycle begins all over again. Do you have any clue what you just read? Probably not. I missed my target audience. Only people who have worked in the Air Force Air Staff would recognize what I was saying.

For you to understand what I wrote above I would have to explain all the acronyms and the budget program and pricing process. A graphic aid, such as a PowerPoint slide, would also help you to understand. By speaking, explaining the terms, and pointing to the chart as I mention the terms and timeframes, the process will make sense.

So, let's try this again and look at the PowerPoint chart on the next page when you think it is appropriate. In developing the Air Force Budget, the Air Staff, which are the program managers for the Air Force, work on the Program Objective Memorandum, aka the POM. The POM is developed in the spring and the POM is where the Program Managers decide what programs to keep. In the summer, we price the POM, but when we price the POM we use the term BES. BES stands for Budget Estimate Submission. Once the pricing of the BES is complete, we submit the PBR to the Office of the Secretary of Defense (OSD) to review. The PBR is the combined POM/BES and PBR stands for Program Budget Review. As you can see, the PBR is an Air Force internal process.

PPBE Overview

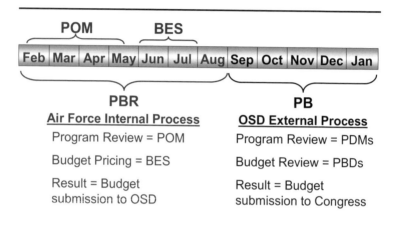

POM   BES

| Feb | Mar | Apr | May | Jun | Jul | Aug | Sep | Oct | Nov | Dec | Jan |

PBR   PB
Air Force Internal Process   **OSD External Process**

Program Review = POM   Program Review = PDMs

Budget Pricing = BES   Budget Review = PBDs

Result = Budget   Result = Budget
submission to OSD   submission to Congress

After we submit the PBR (the combined POM/BES) to OSD in the September timeframe, we close the PBR and open the PB exercise. The PB is the President's Budget and it is an OSD externally driven process. All the changes will come in the form of PDMs (Program Decision Memorandums) and PBDs (Program Budget Decisions). PBDs and PDMs normally happen in the Nov-Dec timeframe. Once we incorporate the PDM and PBD changes into the PB, then we will submit our revised PB back to OSD in January and in February, we start the whole Planning, Programming, Budgeting, and Execution (PPBE) cycle back over again.

Let's look at our takeaways.

You always have to be aware of your audience. What you say and how you convey your topic are very important. Knowing your audience involves doing some homework. What does your audience want to see and hear? Does your boss like briefings in color? Or black and white? At a senior level view? An in-depth in-the-weeds view? How should you dress? You don't want to wear a suit to a NASCAR race and you don't want to wear a pair of Speedos to the company formal either. Does your audience know the acronyms you are using? Does the audience even care about what you are saying? How do you attract the audience's attention? What words and actions do you need to refrain from doing so as not to offend the audience? Don't talk above the level of the audience, remember KISS-Keep it Simple Stupid. KISS works. What about training aids?

A great leader adjusts his delivery, presentation style, speech, training aids, and content depending on who he is talking to in order to connect with the audience. The way you talk to your boss will be different than how you talk with your junior employees. The way you talk to your teammates is different than how you talk to your mother. Always, always, always know your audience!

Sometimes the hardest people to talk with are our family members. If your spouse or children feel like you are talking down to them, you have lost your audience. If you don't know what interests them, you can't relate to them and will lose your audience. It can be so frustrating for you because you expect them to listen and understand you because they are your family.

Here are some words of wisdom. You actually have to work harder to know your family than to know and understand your co-workers and friends. Your spouse and each of your kids, most likely, will be motivated by different means of communication, such as quality time, physical touch, words of affirmation, or receiving gifts. A good book that describes these communication techniques is "The 5 Love Languages" by Gary Chapman.

As a father/husband, what do your children/spouse want? When was the last time you sat down with your child/spouse and asked them what is important to them? When was the last time you actually listened to what they had to say and not come up with excuses as to why you didn't meet the need? How can you help them if you really don't even know who they are?

As a coach, you are fortunate enough to have people that have a common desire in a sport to help you grab their attention, but you still have to motivate them. A group of high school boys most likely will not be interested in getting rewarded with ice cream. Military or sports stories of encouragement can inspire them. Being on the starting team may be a good motivator for some. Being on a winning team is motivational for many people. The threat of corrective training for substandard performance can be a motivator. Praise for doing well is another motivator. Learn your players. Talk with them. Make going over the playbook fun. Find a way.

So, how do you find out what your audience wants? Determine who your audience is and then ask them or someone that knows them well. For example, ask your boss's secretary, his number 2, or a person that briefs the boss regularly. Talk with your subordinates/teammates/children everyday to find out what motivates them. And let us not forget to use common sense.

Are you connecting with your audience or is it in one ear and out the other? Have you done your homework on what and who you are briefing? Have you tried to get in your audiences' shoes to see their perspective on what you are talking about? Are you talking in a "language" your audience understands? If not, you have missed your target audience.

Chapter 12

Developing Others

When I was in the Army, a Brigade Commander (BDE CDR) held the rank of Colonel (COL) and was in charge of 3-4 battalions. A Battalion Commander (BN CDR) held the rank of Lieutenant Colonel (LTC) and was in charge of 3-6 companies depending on the type of battalion. Each battalion was made up of 300-1,000 Soldiers. In relation to the civilian sector, a BDE CDR is equivalent to a CEO in charge of 3-4 separate organizations and a BN CDR is equivalent to a vice president/ regional director of an organization.

So how do you develop younger leaders who show potential?

Situation 1, Recognize potential

My second BN CDR over the objections of the BDE CDR made a young officer in the rank of 2nd Lieutenant (the lowest officer rank) who was soon to pin on 1st Lieutenant rank the Battalion Operations Officer for the largest battalion in the entire 82nd Airborne Division. This was unheard of! The BN CDR picked this lieutenant over a seasoned captain to perform the job that managed the daily operations and the long-term planning of this unit.

Why did the BN CDR take this risk? He saw potential in the lieutenant and wanted to mold that lieutenant into a better officer. How did the lieutenant feel about it? The lieutenant felt honored to be chosen for such a responsible position, felt loyalty to the BN CDR to do the best job he could, and the lieutenant felt valued. What were the results? The lieutenant exceeded everyone's expectations, filled the job for 21 months (normally held for 12 months or less), the battalion thrived, and the lieutenant became a much more valuable leader to the Army.

Now, I left out a few critical facts. The BN CDR mentored the lieutenant. How did he do that? Many, many different ways. One way was he gave the lieutenant enough rope to do great things, but not enough rope to hang himself with. In other words, the BN CDR gave the lieutenant power, but not unchecked power.

For major projects, the BN CDR would give the lieutenant ideas of what he wanted the lieutenant to do and then told the lieutenant about some resources he might want to use. The lieutenant would then develop a product that the BN CDR would review before the project was put into action.

Another great way the BN CDR developed the lieutenant was he backed up the decisions the lieutenant made. In other words, the BN CDR gave the lieutenant the AUTHORITY and the RESPONSIBILITY to perform his job. This was critical. If the BN CDR had overridden the decisions of the lieutenant, the lieutenant would have failed in his job.

One more way the BN CDR developed the lieutenant is that they would go to breakfast or lunch together a few times a week along with other staff members in order that everyone could share ideas and he could impart wisdom to his staff.

Finally, who was that young lieutenant? It was me and I learned so much and rose to a much higher level professionally because of this experience. Not only did I benefit, but the organization did too as I became the backbone of the organization amidst the change of two BN CDRs, three executive officers (vice presidents), three support officers, four budget officers, four personnel officers, and fifteen company commanders!

So what is the point here? Every great leader develops and trains new leaders in the organization. And as leaders are empowered, the organization will thrive. A great leader works himself out of a job by training others, which installs a legacy, which in turn allows the great leader to move to the next level to develop others.

Do you develop others or do you have to do everything yourself because no one else can do it as good as you (This is a big trap a lot of people fall into)? Do you empower your subordinates/teammates/children or do you override their decisions on a regular basis? Are you building a team that can operate successfully in your absence or when you are not there, the organization fails to operate well?

As a leader, you must evaluate at what level your children/team/employees are currently operating at before you can begin to develop them properly. This comes from proper counseling (See Chapter 5, Counseling). In so doing, you will have to make a judgment call of how much you get involved with helping a subordinate. For those that aren't that mature and don't have any or many skills, you tell them what to do and watch over them. For those that are more mature and have some skills, you give some guidelines and interject guidance as needed. For those that are mature and have a lot of skills, you guide them in conversation and encourage them to come up with solutions.

In other words, the level of guidance and latitude a leader doles out, depends on the competence of the individual, level of experience, and the situation at hand.

Note: I believe it is better to have motivated employees that want to learn than an expert who knows it all and is not a team player.

So, let's look at some situations to help you out.

Situation 2, Immature/mature person with no skills (Computer example)

When you first learn how to use a computer program, the instructor walks and talks you step-by-step through the computer program and has a handout for you listing step-by-step what you must do. So, the instructor tells you what to do and you do it.

Situation 3, Immature/mature person with no skills (Weapon example)

When learning how to fire a weapon, the instructor will teach you the safety rules first. Then he will tell you how to perform each step in firing a weapon. Once you have mastered each step, you will practice "dry" firing the weapon (no ammunition). Finally, the instructor, while watching you like a hawk, will allow you to fire the weapon. Just as with the computer example, the instructor tells you what to do and you do it.

So, for your new "fresh" employees/children/players, you must teach them the basic tasks. They don't learn it by themselves; you teach them the right way.

Situation 4, Mature person with some skills

You have an employee that is responsible and possesses some computer skills. You need a spreadsheet report about how the organization is doing on training. Instead of telling him how to fill in every cell and how big each cell must be, which would demotivate your employee, you instead give the guidelines of, "The report must be compatible with the other report formats we have so information is easy to transfer in and out (user friendly), the report must have _____ information as a minimum, and use your judgment for anything else."

Nine times out of ten, the product the employee develops, with minor modifications (teaching points), will be just what you needed and even more important, you will have developed a much more capable employee.

The mature and some skills individual is the person you want to start putting in leadership positions and giving greater responsibility. Give him enough rope to do great things, but not enough rope to hang himself. Big decisions must come to you first. Keep regular developmental counseling going strong.

Situation 5, Mature person with a lot of skills

Minimal guidance is needed for the mature person with a lot of skills. Assign the task and let him develop the solutions with minimal input from you.

Situation 6, Immature person with some or a lot of skills

These are the most dangerous people to an organization/team/family. These people tend to care about themselves first, but if willing to grow, they can become some of your best employees through proper counseling and discipline (See Chapter 5, Counseling and Chapter 6, Discipline).

Those that refuse your instruction are best to be removed from the organization. You can't change all people. Now, if you can't remove these immature people, assign them menial tasks at or below their skill level, hold them accountable for their actions, and put motivated, mature individuals with some or a lot of skills in their place. The motivated, mature people are rewarded and the immature people may begin to grow up, but if not, at least their harm is minimized.

Let's talk a little about negative correction/fixing problems.

Situation 7, Counseling when have a problem, Immature/mature person with no skills

For an employee/player/child who does not possess many skills in the problem area, you have to show him what the problem is, hold the person accountable, provide the solution/perform the discipline (if disciplinary problem), oversee the solution, and then treat the issue as past, unless/until it happens again.

One of my Soldiers, Sergeant (SGT) G went on a mission and drove on unsafe roads, where if he was in an accident and died, none of his benefits would be passed to his family because he went on this mission against my orders. SGT

G chose to listen to another leader not responsible for him instead of me.

When SGT G got back from his mission, I called him into my office and I asked him a couple of questions in a calm, relaxed manner.

Me: "SGT G, do you understand what red road conditions mean?"

SGT G: "No, Sir."

Me: "Do you know what would happen if you got injured while disobeying a direct order?"

SGT G: "No, Sir."

Me: "Were you absolutely clear that I had forbid you to perform this mission?"

SGT G: "Yes, Sir."

Me: "SGT G. I am going to give you the command to stand at attention in just a moment, because I want you to fully understand that I am serious. Are we clear?"

SGT G: "Yes, Sir."

Me: "Position of attention, move." SGT G moved to the position of attention. I changed the tone of my voice to firm. "SGT G, unless someone higher ranking than me tells you to do something contrary to my order, then I will hold you accountable for your actions. Do you understand?"

SGT G: "Yes, Sir."

Me: Still in a firm tone (but now as a loving father's concerned voice tone), "Because you are my responsibility, I am going to discipline you. You have the potential to be an outstanding leader, but you need to learn the rules so I can count on you and develop you. Now, stand at, ease."

I pause for effect and then continue, "SGT G, it is because I care about you that I am disciplining you. Let me tell you about how I discipline my daughter."

"When my daughter does something wrong, I don't raise my voice and yell angrily at her. Instead, I make sure I am calm and then call her over. I then have her tell me what she did that was wrong and if she doesn't know or hesitates, I prompt her. I then calmly and firmly tell her why it was wrong and that because I love her, I am not going to tolerate that behavior. I then discuss our method to correct the behavior. Finally, after administering the discipline, I hug my daughter and tell her I love her. The problem is then over and we go about our business as if nothing had happened."

Smiling I say, "Now, don't worry, I am not going to tell you I love you and hug you." SGT G laughs.

I continue, "But I do care for you and I take my responsibility seriously, so I will discipline you. SGT G, do you understand the difference between discipline and punishment?"

SGT G: (Looking confused) "No, Sir."

Me: "Punishment is you did something wrong, you got caught, and now you will pay the price. Discipline is you did something wrong, you got caught, and we take steps to correct your negative behavior."

SGT G: "I think I get it."

Me: "Good. Now, I am going to put you at attention and administer the discipline. As soon as that is over, then it will be as this never happened. Position of attention, move."

"So you have no confusion as to who your chain of command is, you will read _____ and report back to me what you find on Monday morning. So you understand what safe and unsafe traffic conditions are, you are going to read the Transportation regulation and write a two-page report on what the different traffic conditions are (green, yellow, red, and black) and what approval is needed to drive in these conditions. The report is due in one week. And so you have time to complete these assignments, you will spend two hours a day after work in the office completing the work. A copy of these assignments is here for you so you don't have to try to remember what I just told you."

"Stand at, ease. What are your questions for me at this time?"

SGT G: "No questions Sir, but it seems a little harsh."

Me: "SGT G. The discipline stands. This is a serious matter, but if you have any questions about this assignment, feel free to ask me anytime. I really do care about you and you truly have the ability to be a great leader. I believe in you. I think you will understand the discipline more after you have completed it. Now don't sulk; everybody makes mistakes. Will you blow it from time-to-time? Of course you will. I know I do. Humble yourself, admit the mistake, correct the mistake, and move on. You have it in you. I can sense greatness in you."

A week later after the discipline was over, SGT G had a much greater respect for what happened and had a small appreciation for the discipline. He saw that I was not out to get him, but to develop him and make him better. This incident and the correction helped to transform our relationship and SGT G himself. Within six months, SGT G truly understood and appreciated the discipline. The changes in his life (on duty and off duty) were so dramatic it was amazing. All it took was loving discipline that he had never had before.

So, for SGT G, I showed him what the problem was, I held him accountable for his actions, and I provided the solution along with overseeing it. Once the discipline was over, it was as if it never happened and with his previous mistake not being used against him, it built his confidence that being good doesn't mean you are perfect.

Situation 8, Counseling when have a problem, mature individual with some skills

For a mature employee with some skills in the problem area, you can't tell him what to do or he will tune you out. You have to lead him into seeing there is a problem (unless he brought the problem to you to discuss) and the two of you work at finding a solution.

You as the leader guide the process and recommend some potential solutions. You then check in regularly to see how progress is being made.

For example, I had a Soldier that was great in everything he did, but he wasn't paying his bills on time. In talking with him, I found out he had never learned how to manage money and didn't know how to use a checkbook. He was also spending a lot of money on things he didn't need. He wanted help so I recommended we get him into a financial management class (I taught him how to use a checkbook in the mean time) and I recommended he stop purchasing things he didn't need at this time. Note: We discussed needs vs. wants and I had him make a list of daily expenditures so he could track his spending and see where his money was going.

At the end of the talk, I told him I was proud of him for recognizing he had a problem and beginning to take steps to overcome it.

Within two months, he was well on his way of getting out of debt and within six months, he was out of debt and saving money too.

Situation 9, Counseling when have a problem, mature individual with a lot of skills

For a mature employee with some skills in the problem area, you are now a facilitator and occasionally integrate thoughts as needed (such as, Did you think about this?...What about that?...Good point...Go on...etc.) so that the mature person develops the solution on his own. Then, you congratulate him on determining the solution and have him get going on implementing the solution.

Many times the mature individual with many skills just needs a sounding board, sometimes they just need your authority, and other times they need a little guidance as listed above.

For example, the vice president of the company comes to the president and says,

VP: "We have a problem. At the rate we are producing, we aren't going to meet the minimum production quota for the month."

P: "What do you think the problem is?"

VP: "Well Sir, we have enough supplies and the machines are working fine. I think the problem is that it takes two hours to manufacture part C instead of one hour and this is the bottleneck of our operation. We underestimated the time it takes to manufacture part C."

P: "And how do you think we should solve this problem?"

VP: "If we pull twenty workers from the other teams, we can cross train them in the skills needed to make part C. Instead of sitting idle waiting for part C to be made, now they can be made productive. Now that I think of it, by doing this, I bet we can meet the production goal five days ahead of schedule at a ten percent savings to the company."

P: "That sounds good, but what about union issues? Do you see any heartburn there?"

VP: "No. No issues if we pass on some of the savings to the workers. I am sure we would get the union's support."

P: "Good idea. Keep me posted on your progress and if you run into any issues I am here to help."

Situation 10, Ranger Challenge team

When I was Captain of the Ranger Challenge team*, I was responsible for all the training for the six events along with planning and executing the trip. The school cadre, led by a senior non-commissioned officer (NCO), purposefully took a "hands-off" approach to develop us as leaders. The NCO would occasionally ask questions like "Did you think of this or that?" to steer us in the right direction and any supplies we asked for, he would get. A little more background, most of my team had never really held a leadership position nor had I myself, but we were competent and motivated.

If I had tried to manage everything myself, we would not have been successful. Instead, I picked team leads for each event and the administrative pieces. I briefed the team leads individually of what I expected from each of them and I had each team lead back brief me (restate what I told them) to ensure we saw eye-to-eye what I wanted accomplished.

When there were issues or better ways of doing things, I would pull the team lead aside and would discuss the points privately, so as not to embarrass them, nor to take away their authority. As we improved, I would praise each leader in front of the team. I would also conduct a weekly thirty minute meeting focused on how the training was going and if there were any issues that developed.

The results in all of us and our team were outstanding. As a team, we took one first, two seconds, and a third against teams that were from bigger schools (more talent pool), military colleges, and who were trained by Special Forces and Ranger instructors (guys who live and breathe these events and are the experts). Each one of us had learned how to lead in front, plan logistics, succeed against the odds, and inspire others to accomplish the mission at hand. When we went to our units upon graduation, all of us were much better prepared than the average officer just out of college because our cadre did not baby us, but instead let us develop as leaders.

*Ranger Challenge. Ranger Challenge consists of constructing a one man rope bridge over water and crossing it, a 12 mile forced march with weapon and back pack weighing 35 lbs, weapons assembly/disassembly, land navigation, a Physical Fitness test, and a written test. The events are conducted over a two day time period. A team is made up of nine members and the top eight scores count.

Situation 11, Coaching

It is very easy to just focus on the star players and develop them. But what if the star player gets hurt? A better strategy for the game and for life is to develop the team and the star player. The coach can use the star player to help train others. As the others get better, their self confidence increases and the team gets better.

As far as the non-athletes go, an even greater focus on teaching the basics to them by one of the coaches for 15-20 minutes can help develop them as players, but more importantly it works on the self confidence they need for life. The non-athlete sees that someone took the time to develop him and what had seemed hopeless only weeks before, now is not quite so bad.

Are you taking the time to develop the next generation leaders? Are you working yourself out of a job? Are you counseling your employees to develop them? Have you identified the maturity/skill level of your employees/players/children? Are you conducting negative counseling if needed (but ending on a positive note)? Are you developing a team or just individuals? Are you seeking development from a leader you respect?

Chapter 13

Delegation of Authority

Situation 1, No delegation

Do you know someone who has to do everything himself so that it is "correct" while the other people in the office have nothing to do? Also notice how that person becomes overwhelmed, begins running late, gets burned out at some point in time, and then blames his problems on the others who weren't helping him out?

Situation 2, Over delegation

Do you know the boss who piles task upon task on all his employees; does nothing himself; does not check up on tasks; and when tasks are not completed on time/to standard, he blames you?

Either of these situations sound familiar?

You can delegate authority, but not responsibility. A good leader recognizes that he can not do everything; there just are not enough hours in the day. Delegating authority frees a leader up to think about the big picture and the direction his organization needs to move in. Now, will everything be done exactly the way you would do it? No. Is that ok? In most instances as long as it meets the standards, "Yes." And many times, you will also find that many of your subordinates' ideas are better than your own!

Now, when you delegate, you can't just forget about the task and not check up on it until it is due from your subordinate. This is a recipe for failure! A perfect example of this that many people do is the "fire and forget" email which is another issue in itself. You also can't just assume a subordinate has the skills or the resources available to accomplish the mission. When we assume, we usually make an **ass** out of **u** and **me**.

So, how do you delegate?

1. State the tasks to be performed, the standards you expect to be met, and when it is due.*
2. Have the subordinate restate what you want done, how you expect it to look, and when it is due.
3. If the subordinate does not restate what you want done correctly, repeat steps 1-2.
4. If you have an example product and can recommend some resources, do so.
5. Confirm the employee has the skills to accomplish the task. If not, take the time to get him started on the right foot.
6. Inform the employee to come to you with any problems he can't solve early, so you have time to help him before it is too late.
7. Ask how your employee is coming along regularly so there are no surprises. You will be amazed at some of the answers you get!
8. If along the way you realize this task is above the subordinate's abilities, take the project away and give to someone who can do it so the mission is still accomplished. Ensure the subordinate that failed gets the corrective training needed.

Note: Sometimes it may be more advantageous to let the subordinate help set the standards and due date to create better "buy in" to the process.

You will notice that the first two steps above involve proper communication between you and the subordinate. I specifically chose the word communication, because both he and you must understand what you want accomplished. Too often, we fail to communicate and we waste good time and money on accomplishing the wrong task or accomplishing nothing at all. Do not simply take an "I understand" or "I got it." Have the subordinate restate what you said to your satisfaction. If you do not, many times the project will not be done to specifications.

Note: Until the subordinate proves himself, leave extra time for you to critique the work and send it back for correction. You don't want to be trying to fix things at the last minute for your turn in to higher.

If your subordinate fails to accomplish his task, you have to hold him responsible if you provided him with the proper resources, checked on him, and the task was reasonable. And when your superior wants to know why the task wasn't performed, you can't blame your subordinate, you have to take the blame. To correct your subordinate's substandard behavior, see Chapter 5, Counseling; Chapter 6, Discipline; and Chapter 12, Developing Others.

Now, if you did not resource your subordinate (set him up for success), learn from your mistake and apologize to the subordinate for your failure in your responsibility to him. If this sounds a lot like leading from the front, it is!

Delegation of authority is great for work, but how do you do it at home? Ah, that is the million dollar question. Each home and family relationship is a little different, but the same principles apply; however, now you and your spouse need to come to agreement on how to attack different situations.

For example, Dad may perform the actual discipline to the boys and Mom for the girls. If Mom lets the girls off scott free for what the boys get in trouble for, however, then Dad and Mom need to have a talk about their responsibility in the discipline they owe the children. You can't send mixed signals.

Situation 2, Family duties

Now, let's say that the husband and wife decide his duties around the house are laundry, dishes, trash, and mowing the lawn. If the husband knows he is going out of town, he still has the responsibility to take care of his chores because his wife is counting on him. He needs to do what he can before going on the trip. If he normally does laundry on Saturday, but he is leaving on Friday and not coming back until Monday, he needs to do the laundry on Thursday. For the lawn, he can coordinate for a neighborhood boy to do it or coordinate with the wife that he will do it on Tuesday when he returns if she does not object. This is called accepting responsibility and showing respect to your spouse.

For your children, you assign them their chores. If you do not check up on them and see how they are coming along on those chores, then their failure to perform their chores is your responsibility also. Remember, you are their leader!

Situation 3, Coach and assistant coaches

Did you notice that most successful sports teams have coaches who delegate authority to the assistant coaches? I was on one such football team in high school.

Before we began training camp, the head coach got with all the assistant coaches and showed the assistant coaches what he wanted them to teach us players. When training camp began, the head coach observed the assistant coaches and he corrected deficient training when needed.

By empowering his assistant coaches to train, it freed the head coach up to evaluate where the team was and adjust the training as appropriate. The end result is that we became the co-champions that year.

Do you delegate responsibility or do you delegate authority? Do you keep all the work to yourself because no one else can do it as well as you? Are you burnt out? Do you really know how to delegate? Ask those that are around you and remember, their perception is reality not yours (Chapter 7, Do as I Say, Not as I Do). Are you giving your subordinates the authority to do their job? If you are delegating authority, are you checking up and setting your employees/family/team and yourself up for success?

Note: A leader that does not delegate is not a leader. He is an overpaid worker in a leadership position.

Chapter 14

Counsel of 2 or 3

Situation 1, Light fixture

The other day I was helping a friend of mine install a new light fixture for her kitchen. I put in the fixture and she watched ☺. This new fixture had two swivel (turning) lights on the end and three center lights. The three center lights could be adjusted 90 degrees.

After the light fixture was installed, she realized that the three center lights were pointed in the opposite direction of where they needed to be. As I was getting ready to unscrew the fixture and flip it around, Darla said, "Why don't you see if the bases of the three center lights move?" Guess what? They did!

Maybe that was common sense, but it also goes back to the rule of two or three. Had Darla not suggested turning the bases, I would have gone down the longer and harder path of taking down the fixture, turning it around, and then reinstalling it. This is a perfect example of how two minds work better than one.

Situation 2, Resume

Another example is you are writing a resume. Once you have finished it, you need to have at least one or two people you respect look at it. Why? There are several reasons.

First, they will find some errors or omissions that you didn't see because you are too close to the subject matter. Secondly, since they have an outside point of view, they can give you objective criticism and provide wise insights you skipped over. Third, we all have different writing and presentation styles so they may take your basic ideas and transform them into a much better laid out product that is also packaged in a more attractive way.

Situation 3, MBA Group

Remember my MBA group? It was made up of five people: Srini, a brown man originally from India who is a computer expert, math genius, and very creative; Derril, a Southern black man who is a computer expert, creative, and always willing to help others; Carla, a Hispanic woman with tremendous writing ability and organization skills; Brenda, a white woman with great writing skills and business sense; and me, a white guy with a military background, presentation skills, and a sense of practicality. We were a very diverse group with completely different backgrounds. Each one of us brought certain strengths to the group.

In completing each of our group projects and presentations, one of us would take the lead and then get input from the others. It never ceased to amaze me how awesome our final product would always be. And do you know why our products were awesome? It was because of the different thinking processes we had, our different backgrounds, and when combined together, we looked at a problem almost every way imaginable. Our diversity was our strength. When one person said one thing, that triggered a thought in someone else's head. Our group product was always better than any one of our individual leads because of the counsel of others and our diversity.

Situation 4, A big operation

In the military, we always created operation orders before performing any significant task. The operation order laid out the tasks to be performed, provided a mission statement (the 5 W's- Who, What, When, Where, Why, and How), explained the logistics, and provided who was in charge.

As the operations officer for my organization, I was responsible for creating the operation order. I would receive inputs from the personnel officer, the budget/supply officer, the intelligence officer, and the support operations officer.

I would then synchronize the information and make sure the information was correct and easy to read. Before I ever sent out an order to subordinate units, I always had my number two in charge check it out and a respected person outside of my office to check it. Why? To ensure readability, common sense, the prevention of errors, and to get an objective third person view. Not only did this make the quality of my work improve, it also improved the relationship of my section with the other sections in our organization and it helped to prevent tunnel vision thinking.

Situation 5, Checking on the basics

Remember back in chapter 4, Taking Care of Others, that my father would check on the troops in the field and at their installations on a regular basis? My dad would make a point to do three things on every visit to an installation which were: Point 1, Check the sanitary conditions to include the restrooms; Point 2, Check on the operations; and Point 3, Talk openly and candidly with the troops (workers).

We didn't discuss Point 3 of how he talked openly and candidly with the troops then, but we will now. This ties into the counsel of 2 or 3 in that at every level of command, a leader has subordinate staff/leaders that advise him on how to run an organization. The counsel of the staff is very important, but a leader must also confirm what his staff is telling him is accurate.

To do this, he has to get out and talk to the front line leaders and the workers at the operational level. The leader has to get candid input from these front line personnel. If the staff answers and the field answers are in synch, the information flow is working well. If the answers are out of synch, then there is a break down between the staff and the front line organizations or worse.

Counsel is important, but it must be checked to prevent tunnel vision, to ensure an organization is in synch, and to promote integrity.

Situation 6, Family issues

Your kids are acting up and you don't know what to do. Or maybe, you think you do, but the results of your actions are anything but spectacular with your kids. You don't have to parent alone!

Seek advice from people that you know are doing or have done a good job raising kids and have the experience to back them up. Maybe, your parents, your spouse's parents, a respected couple in your church, and/or a good self help book like "Bringing Up Boys" by Dr. James Dobson or "The New Strong Willed Child."

Situation 7, Facing the Giants kicker

In the movie, "Facing the Giants" there was a kicker who had no self confidence. His father gave him the guidance that what one believes, his actions will follow. Then an assistant coach helped him to picture how to kick a field goal. Finally, the head coach told the kicker he had faith in him and then the kicker made what would have seemed an impossible field goal. The counsel of 2 or 3 turned around an insecure boy and had him accomplish a task most men could not do.

Do you try to do everything yourself? When was the last time you asked for a second opinion to your idea? If you are using the counsel of two or three, are you occasionally checking with others to make sure you have good counselors? Are you counseling others or keeping your knowledge to yourself?

Remember, one person does not have a lock on all good ideas. Therefore, it is essential that you run your ideas by others to ensure your ideas are: valid, on target, big picture, and not disastrous. Your counselors can also build upon your good idea and turn it into a great action.

Chapter 15

Big Picture vs. Tunnel Vision

For today's reading please also include Chapter 16, Team vs. Self Mentality. These two chapters are very closely related.

Situation 1, Acquisition

The Vice-President of Acquisition was all excited. He had just bought $100 million worth of computers for only $75 million and thus saved the company $25 million. He couldn't wait to tell the president of the company. After he briefed the president, the president asked a couple of questions. "Are these new computers compatible with Systems B & C and are the computers upgradeable with future platforms?" The smile and enthusiasm of the vice-president turned to a look of horror. He had just purchased a legacy system that would not support the needs of the company in the future. Instead of saving $25 million, he wasted $75 million.

Situation 2, Leadership in action

A friend of mine works for an organization that has seven different departments. His department, let's call it the operations department, is responsible for getting the right person with the right skills to the right place on time. If this does not happen, the company does not get paid and fails in its mission. The other six departments all contribute to this candidate processing (security checks, medical, human resources, etc.).

Now, remember, for the company to be successful, it must get the right candidate to the right place at the right time with the right skills. You would think that the other six departments would be focused on supporting the operations department to maximize the number of candidates, but they don't. Each of the other department heads want their fiefdom to perform at 100% even at the expense of the other sections. Now, if the operations department can only operate at 60% because of the lack of teamwork, does it matter that the other sections perform at 100%. No! The operations department drives the revenue!

If the other departments would work with the operations department to reach the company's goal, then the teamwork would translate into more revenue and a better work environment for all. These department heads lack vision of how their piece fits into the overall picture of the company and this makes the company under perform. The president of the company is also at fault for not seeing the big picture. And if he does see the big picture, he is at fault for not reeling his leaders in to support the big picture of winning as an organization.

A leader must always look at the big picture and understand it first before making decisions. A great deal today of your role in the organization must be looked at in the context of the big picture. A leader is responsible for providing vision to his organization, team, or family. Once the leader understands the intent of his boss (and his boss's boss), then the leader can inspire his own people to accomplish their part of the mission in the greater scheme of the organization's mission.

Are you putting your team ahead of the company's mission or are you working as a team to support the company's mission? Do you think how your actions will positively or negatively affect the future and can your positive actions be built upon? What is your role in the big picture of things?

Situation 3, Global vision with local action

Another way to describe the concept of vision is to "think globally, act locally." What does that mean to you? For example, you want to travel the world in 80 days. Your vision is that you hike in Antarctica, cross a desert in Africa, canoe in South America, and walk on the Great Wall of China. To be successful, you have to think locally. What clothes will you wear at the North Pole? The desert? In the jungle? On the great wall? What type of money will you use? What type of electricity will you use? Do you need a transformer? Do they even have electricity in some of these locations? Can you drink the water without getting sick? Do you need translators? Etc, etc, etc. It is great to have vision, but for your vision to become successful you must have/create the proper foundation.

Situation 4, Building a leader

When I was a 2nd lieutenant and still new to my unit, my company commander (CO CDR), the senior leader of our 120 person unit, wanted me to create a map overlay consisting of roads, checkpoints, and some unit locations. He gave me absolutely no guidance and I thought, "Yeah, this is easy. I can knock it out in no time!" and that is what I did. I cut a piece of acetate (overlay material) and taped it to the map board. I then got a big, fat, black marker and traced all the roads so it would be no problem to identify the roads. Finally, I drew in the check points and the unit locations. I was done in less than 20 minutes and I was proud of myself!

I went to the CO CDR and said I had that map overlay he wanted completed and he could inspect it. Now, the commander knew the map overlay he asked for could not be done to standard in that amount of time and he asked me, "Has the First Sergeant (1SG, the highest non-commissioned officer in the unit) seen it yet?" "No Sir." "Run it by the 1SG and when he approves of it, come see me." "Yes Sir," I responded. Note: Our 1SG was the most tactical and technically proficient non-commissioned officer I have ever worked with.

I went to the 1SG and asked him if he could take a few minutes to check out my map overlay and he said, "Sure Sir." When we got to the map board and he saw my overlay, he managed not to laugh. The 1SG then looked at me and said in a very professional way, "Sir, I went to the Battle Staff Course where we spent 6 weeks learning how to properly create map overlays" and he paused (for effect I think, and that is what it did to me- 6 weeks of schooling for a map overlay! I knew right then and there that my overlay was jacked up!). Before the 1SG could say anything else, I asked him if he would be willing to share some of his wisdom and teach me. The 1SG's eyes lit up and he said he would be glad to. First, he gave me some reference materials to read and then told me to get back with him.

I ended up getting back with the 1SG quite a few times as I prepared the overlay and he would give me tips and tricks of what to do and where to look for answers. He also gave me the proper pens and other materials to create a professional overlay.

Three or four days afterwards and at least a good 15 hours of work and research later, the 1SG blessed off on my work. I then boldly informed the CO CDR that the map overlay was complete, 1SG approved it, and the overlay was ready for his inspection. The commander then inspected it, gave me his approval, sat me down to glean the lessons learned from this experience, and then he taught me how to brief an overlay.

There are so many lessons of leadership that can be taken from this example, but I will just mention a few. First, my CO CDR did not give me any guidance whatsoever! The commander did this for two reasons. He not only wanted to see what ideas I would come up with on my own (He did not limit my creativity at first), but he also wanted to see if I knew how to use my resources (Why do things the hard way and blindly on your own? Someone, somewhere in your organization has experience and can help you). Note: This project had the time for this no initial guidance leadership approach.

The second main point is the CO CDR wanted me to use the chain of command. The 1SG needs to know everything going on in the company. I had skipped the chain of command and by doing so, I made the 1SG blind and I WASTED my commander's time. The reason there is a 2nd in charge is because he serves as a quality control point for what goes to the boss (the boss is the final quality control check, not the first) and the 2nd in charge manages the day-to-day. The boss's time is precious and needs to be focused on the big picture.

The third main point is the 1SG instructed me. I humbled my pride and learned while a key leader took time out of his busy schedule to develop a young leader. The 1SG could have kept his control and power by not sharing his knowledge. Instead, he empowered me to become a better leader. Note: The 1SG had me read the standards first (would take initiative on my part) and then when I had a base knowledge of understanding, he instructed me.

The fourth main point is when the map overlay was complete, the CO CDR sat me down and explained why he put me through this process. It was so that I could learn the points above and now that I knew how to create and read map overlays, the commander could teach me how to professionally brief map overlays to superiors and subordinates alike which is exactly what he had me do.

The CO CDR had a vision, he saw the big picture. In order to reach the big picture of me being able to brief a map overlay, the commander had to first make sure I learned the basics. Once I could handle the basics, then I could handle the next level, briefing senior leaders.

Are you only focused on how you and your section perform instead of how your department fits in with the organization's goals? Are you only focused on the here and now instead of planning for the future?

Situation 5, Defense

A football team is playing man-to-man coverage and everyone is guarding their man. The ball is given to the running back who has crossed the line of scrimmage. A player on defense that has tunnel vision will still guard his man instead of seeing the big picture and going after the running back (where the play is).

Situation 6, Practice

During a scrimmage practice, a good coach will occasionally yell, "Stop! Remain where you are!" Then he will ask the players what they are doing, where are they supposed to be, and to take a look around. The players now see the big picture when just a moment ago they did not.

Situation 7, Business owner

How about the business owner who only hires people at the lowest wage possible? Is he going to attract the best employees for long? No, the employees are going to leave and get better salaries as soon as they can. If the owner had vision, he would pay competitive wages or better wages to his employees to instill loyalty and reduce employee turnover. Instead, the owner is blinded by the tunnel vision that shows he has a lower up front cost, but he misses the big picture that the turn-over actually costs more: time lost in training new employees; workers being less motivated because they don't feel taken care of; and most importantly, the loss of institutional knowledge.

Situation 8, Airplane bathroom.

I was on a flight one time and many people used the bathroom. Many people used the paper towels provided, but left the dirty towels on the sink even though the garbage can was empty. It was disgusting!

Each person focused only on himself and left his mess. Ten people later, you couldn't even use the sink. This focus on self (tunnel vision) hurt all passengers (big picture) and is one reason flight costs have gone up.

Situation 9, Scheduling

Ben: "John, when should we schedule the monster truck show?"

John: "How about three weeks from now?"

Ben: "Sounds good to me."

Three weeks later on Mother's Day and hardly anyone is at the monster truck show they wonder why they didn't have a better turn out.

When you plan an event, you must look at the calendar to see what else is going on. You can't just look at any calendar though. You need to look at organization events, local events, and national events that can have a negative/positive impact on what you are planning. The tunnel vision is focusing on your event only versus looking at the big picture (all the other events) and seeing how the big picture affects you.

Situation 10, Computer system replacement

There is an organization that is trying to replace a legacy computer system, not because it doesn't work, but because it is not user-friendly. The old system is command based instead of being a windows menu driven system; thus, when initially learning the legacy system, it is tough.

In developing the replacement system, the organization wanted it to be user-friendly and not only replace the legacy system, but also replace three other legacy systems as well. It was an ambitious project to say the least.

As the programmers began developing the new system, they did not seek input from end users, thus the end users' knowledge was not incorporated. Two years and $50 million in to the project, the system can only interface with one of the legacy systems it is supposed to replace; it can only handle one quarter of the legacy system data; and it takes two-and-a-half times longer! Worse yet, the main system the new one is supposed to replace, already interfaces with the other three systems.

The managers of the program refused to stop funding it because, "We have already put $50 million into it and we need to get our money out of it." These managers are blinded by the sunk cost, which you can never recover, and can't see the big picture. They are now throwing good money away after bad money. Furthermore, the new system, if it ever will work, still does not interact with the organization's higher units, so it will still miss the mark.

Situation 11, Alignment of rewards

If we want our organization to succeed in the long-term (big picture), then the organization must align it's reward system to the success of the organization. All too often, this is not the case. Our society now focuses on rewarding individuals. We want our individual section to perform at its best and we get a big reward when it does- whether it is money, promotions, or praise. This does not encourage teamwork between sections.

Don't get me wrong. It is good to have your section/ team perform the best it can, however, if it does so at the expense of the organization, then you are hurting the organization! We fail to grasp that. Thus, if we want our organization to succeed in the long-term (the big picture), then we need to align our rewards to what causes the organization as a whole to succeed. I will offer some specific ideas on how to properly align rewards in the next chapter.

Keeping the big picture in mind when scheduling events, have you checked the calendar to see if events conflict? When changing a process or a system, have you checked with the end users for their input? Have you laid the foundations to build the big picture? How does your work fit into the big picture for the organization? Are you/your leaders/your subordinates/your peers working to your section's goals at the expense of the organization? Do you ever stop to evaluate where you are at to see if you/your team/your family are in synch with the big picture? Does the reward system in your organization/family/team favor the reward of individuals over the success of the unit?

Chapter 16

Team vs. Self Mentality

Situation 1, Meeting with peers and superiors

If some subordinate organization hasn't sent you the data needed for a briefing, don't dime them out in the meeting! If the boss asks, "Where is so and so?" then you can state the subordinate organization failed to turn in the info. This is different than diming people out.

Diming people out on purpose and in front of others is bad for an organization, creates a climate of distrust, and creates an atmosphere of hostility.

If someone habitually does not send you what is required, talk to them one-on-one. If that does not solve it and/or some good peer pressure does not solve the problem, go to your boss for help. Be up front with him about the good, the bad, and the ugly concerning the situation so he can make an objective decision and when he speaks to the other person, he won't be blindsided by anything the other person says. If blindsided, you lose your credibility.

Situation 2, Extreme Salaries

Salaries of leaders in the past had traditionally been 10-20% higher than that of the workers. Now, in the last twenty-five years, many senior leaders' salaries, stock options, and bonuses are astronomically higher than that of the workers. The justification for the higher compensation is that the company will not attract great leaders if it doesn't have astronomical compensation for senior leaders. How is it working? Not too well overall.

These high paid leaders are rewarded for earning short-term profits for the company. Do they have any incentive to do what is right for the long-term benefit of the company? For the most part, the answer is emphatically, "No!" In fact, the news almost always has stories about these so called "leaders" and the problems caused by them. Just look at Enron or Fannie Mae. The current reward system favors selfish leading.

If you want leaders to act as a team, they must be rewarded as a team. If we want the organization to survive for the long-term, we need to align the rewards to long-term performance. So, how do we align the rewards to reward teamwork/the big picture? Good question. A couple of thoughts are:

1. If the organization as a whole does not meet its target goal (sales quota/performance ranking/customer satisfaction/etc.), then no bonuses/rewards to individuals or sections even if the person/section exceeded expectations.
2. Senior leadership must be seen as rewarding teamwork and not just individuals. The leader who excels at the expense of the other sections is not rewarded with promotion/praise/or raise, but reprimanded instead.
3. Recognize not just the leader with a bonus or award, but the section. Note and example: The leader should not get a $10,000 reward and the workers a $100 reward. The leaders should be rewarded no more than 20% more than the workers. We want to inspire the team!
4. Weekly meetings (2 minutes or less on this subject) using a bubble-chart that is color coded (green-good, amber- warning, red- need help, black- failing) to see where a section is in their part of making the overall organization goal. If green, no discussion merited. If amber, red, or black discussion as required so organization can adjust as needed. Note: This is where other sections can aid if needed. A good section leader will have

coordinated for this help before the meeting and then make mention of it during the meeting (rewarding with praise his peer section for help which lets the senior leadership sees that the other section assisted and helps them to reward teamwork as mentioned in point 2 above.).

5. Three-tiered rewards when organization as a whole meets its target goal (sales quota/performance ranking/customer satisfaction/etc.). Tier one reward, bonus everyone gets for meeting the goal. Tier-two reward, bonus sections get for making/exceeding their section goals for the organization. Tier-three reward, bonus for teamwork between sections to make organization goal. Note: The tier-three reward may exceed the tier-two reward because a section may not have met its own goals in order to help another section so the organization as a whole would meet its goal.

Situation 3, Teamwork

In the previous chapter, we looked at a dysfunctional organization from a tunnel vision perspective and briefly alluded to the teamwork part. Now, I want us to hone in on this same organization from a teamwork perspective. Keep in the back of your mind, an organization that is divided against itself is doomed to failure.

So, we have seven different departments. One department, the operations department, is responsible for getting the right person with the right skills to the right place on time. If this does not happen, the company does not get paid and fails in its mission. The other six departments all contribute to this candidate processing (security checks, medical, human resources, etc.).

Now, remember, for the company to be successful, it must get the right candidate to the right place at the right time with the right skills. You would think that the other six departments would be focused on supporting the operations department to maximize the number of candidates, but they don't. Each of the other department heads wants their fiefdom to perform at 100% even at the expense of the other sections. Why? One of the reasons is they are rewarded for their department being the best. Another reason is there is no incentive (no reward) to operate their section at 90% if need be so that the organization will win. In fact, these leaders would be punished (mediocre evaluations, smaller bonuses, and no bragging rights about their greatness) instead of being rewarded. But let's think about this.

If the operations department can only operate at 60% because of the lack of teamwork, does it matter that the other sections perform at 100%. No! The operations department drives the revenue! If the other departments would work with the operations department to reach the company's goal, then the teamwork would translate into more revenue and a better work environment for all. These department heads lack vision of how their piece fits into the overall picture of the company and this makes the company under perform. What we have here is a classic goal alignment problem.

Teamwork is essential in every part of the organization. Our people have to be constantly reminded that we win or lose as a team. The awards also need to be aligned to support the team in addition to individual awards. Within each of your sections, the "I don't like him, so that can wait" attitude has to disappear. You as a leader have to build trust. Teamwork will fail if there is no trust in their workers or leaders. You and your fellow leaders must build trust and work together as a team also.

Now, another big part of motivating a team is understanding the big picture. Once the leader understands the intent of his boss (and his boss's boss), then the leader can inspire his own people to accomplish their part of the mission in the greater scheme of the organization's mission.

Are you putting your team ahead of the company's mission or are you working as a team to support the company's mission? Do you think how your actions will affect the future and can your actions be built upon? What is your role in the big picture of things? Remember, an organization that is divided against itself is doomed to failure.

Situation 4, Basketball team

You have a team with one "superstar" player. He can do it all and he does it by himself every game. He is a star, but the team loses every game. The other players wonder why they even show up. Morale on the team is low. What do you do, Coach?

Build a team! Pull that star player aside and tell him you need him to become a leader, not just a player and if he doesn't listen, bench him. Have him help teach the other players to play better. Build passing plays. Master the basics. Within a few weeks, you can have a much more competitive team and you have developed leaders. And as an added benefit, a team that knows the basics will do better than a team of "hot shots" who don't play together.

Want real life examples? Look at Michael Jordan and the Chicago Bulls, "Magic" Johnson and the LA Lakers, and Larry Bird and the Boston Celtics. The above mentioned players were superstars in their own right, but when coupled with selfless teamwork the teams rose to new levels and it was awesome to watch. Conversely, look at the US Olympic basketball team of 2004. The 2004 all-star team played as individuals and lost more games in one season than all the other US all-star teams *combined* had lost in previous Olympiads! Build a team, not individuals.

Situation 5, Your family

When my wife came home from work today, she still had all the stress from the day with her. I was boiling water in a saucepan in which I would add some noodles. My wife, saw the saucepan and the small bag of noodles and instantly got angry. She raised her voice and said, "You need to use the right pan for the right job." And then proceeded to swap out the hot saucepan with a cold pan while I looked at her thinking, "What is your problem?" and getting upset because she embarrassed me in front of our daughter.

Tricia, still angry, then left the kitchen. I, still a little bit angry myself, left the kitchen and went to the dining room to collect my thoughts and work on the computer some. About five minutes later, Tricia had come downstairs and went into the kitchen. I followed her in. I then asked Tricia to stop for a second and I came over and hugged her. Then we looked into each other's eyes, I kissed her, told her I loved her, and then left the room. I knew that by us hugging, we couldn't stay angry at one another. A few minutes later, Tricia talked about how her day went and I listened. Now unwound, Tricia apologized to Kathleen and myself about how she had acted.

Tricia and I had a choice. It could be about our own individual self or the family. Instead of reacting to Tricia's anger, which was my right, I walked away. Instead of yelling back at Tricia, I hugged her. Instead of letting pride get in the way and justifying her behavior, Tricia apologized. We chose to be a team. Afterwards, I told our daughter how awesome it was that Tricia had apologized and how lucky we are to have her in our lives and Kathleen responded with pride and joy, "I know."

It is hard to be a team when everything inside you wants to lash out in anger. Anything worth having is worth sacrificing for. The highest amount of stress for a lot of families is when a spouse comes home from work and the spouse hasn't had time to wind down. Recognize this and plan accordingly so the family wins.

Do you work for your own rewards at the expense of the organization? Do you reward team performance versus only individual performance? Do you excel at the expense of others in the organization? Do you enjoy diming people out? Are you a hot shot or are you a team player? Do you reward based on short-term performance even if it is at the expense of long-term success for the organization? Is your family a second thought and/or a whipping post or is it a team? Do you put your family first ahead of your needs?

Chapter 17

Styles of Leadership

Every MBA program talks about the risk-adverse leader, the risk-taker, the conflict-avoider, and the confrontational leader, but I want to take a different approach and share with you some different leadership style aspects.

Situation 1, The yeller

"My way or the highway!" your boss says yelling or "I could snap you in two with my fingers if I wanted. Don't get on my bad side." Or how about, "I could fire you right now if I wanted to!" A leader that always yells and threatens is a leader that leads by fear. This is one of the most worthless styles of leadership. This creates an uncomfortable work environment. Employee morale is low. Subordinates do not want to spend any time with the leader. This type of leadership actually *costs* the company money because of the high turnover rates, high absenteeism, legal complaints (it only takes one), and low productivity over the long run.

Note: There are two times to yell. One time is if there is a mistake that can cause injury to life or limb, then yell to stop the event or get someone moving. The other time to raise your voice is if something serious has happened and you need to grab everyone's attention. Since you rarely ever raise your voice like this, your subordinates will quickly turn to you. Now that you have their attention, speak *to* them not *at* them.

Situation 2, The pushover

The pushover leader rarely has original ideas of his own and will go along with the plan that is presented to him last or presented by the person who intimidates him the most. The pushover leader may also be characterized by never being able to say "no" to supervisors even when he knows better.

Situation 3, The dictator

In everything you do, the dictator tells you exactly how he wants everything and leaves no room for ingenuity on your part. There is a time and place for this, such as in danger or a special presentation that has to be perfect, but for every day operations this will demotivate your people. Your people need to have the opportunity to be heard and look at problems from a different point of view other than just your point of view.

Situation 4, The guider/motivator

The guider/motivator is characterized by talking with his employees, asking them how they are doing, providing ideas on solving problems, and encouraging employees. A guider/ motivator provides purpose, motivation, and direction. A guider/motivator is careful not to talk down to, but instead builds up employees to reach new levels of performance.

Situation 5, The micro-manager

The micro-manager is the boss that is always over your shoulder watching and controlling every move you make. The micro-manager has his hands in everything because he does not know how or will not delegate. While the micro-manager may be very successful in the short-term, in the long-term, the micro-manager causes high frustration and high turn-over.

Situation 6, If it ain't broke, don't fix it

This is a very dangerous philosophy that is characterized by the status quo. The only thing constant is change. There is always someone else who can do it better, cheaper, and faster than you can. If you remain constant, you will be left behind. There are times, though, when if it ain't broke, don't fix it. A good leader has to evaluate when and where to apply this philosophy.

So, whenever you hear, "This is the way we have always done it," bells should be going off in your mind. If after questioning this philosophy and it holds up, mark down the reason(s) it held up and revisit anytime the reason(s) change.

Situation 7, Quid pro quo leadership (this for that)

When I was deployed to Iraq, I overheard a logistician (person who provides supplies or services to the warfighter) tell a warfighter (the troop fighting the battle) that he wouldn't help the warfighter unless the warfighter did something for him. I was shocked. When someone needs your help and you have to "make a profit" off them instead of doing the job that you are paid to do, you are a disgrace to your organization. This is a shameful type of leadership. This is quid pro quo leadership at its worst.

Situation 8, Never say no leadership

One of my old bosses taught me this trick. Never tell the people you support, "No, I can't do that." No is negative and turns people away.

Instead, say, "If you want me to do that, it will come at the expense of such and such." This way you are giving them alternatives. It is also at this point you can now offer your own alternatives if you have a better idea of how to meet the needs of your customer and your customer will receive the idea and believe you really are trying to support him. It creates a win-win situation for everyone.

I have also found this style of leadership to be particularly effective in non-life threatening issues with children when modified slightly. For example, you don't want your children to do certain things. Instead of saying, "No, you can't do that." Tell them, "You can do that, however, if you do that the consequence will be _____." Or, you can add in a reward for a substitute behavior by saying words to the effect of, "I don't want you to do _____. If you do that against my wishes, then the consequence will be _____. However, if you choose to do

_____ instead, then I will reward you with _____ (something they consider a reward)." Empower the child to make a decision. More often than not, he will make the right one. More importantly, though, the child is learning to realize there are consequences for the decisions he makes.

Situation 9, The selfish leader

The selfish leader puts himself first at the expense of others. He will work people into the ground and he will do anything to get ahead. What the selfish leader does not understand is that if he put the same energy into taking care of others, they would take care of him.

Note: The selfish leader frequently produces well in the short-term, but the long-term effects are dangerous for all levels of the organization touched by a leader like this. We all have this trait of selfish leading at times, but must recognize it and avoid it. A transformed selfish leader can become one of your best leaders.

Situation 10, Frog and complacency

A frog will hop out of a boiling pot of water if put in. However, if a frog is put in lukewarm water and the temperature is turned up slowly to boiling, the frog will not notice the change and be cooked!

A leader must constantly evaluate his leadership style. Different people require different types of leadership. A leader that does not recognize this will suffocate his organization/team/ or family without ever even knowing it.

Now, the frog is an example of complacency. Because the changes around you seem minor, you do not adjust. A leader that does not have the vision nor the courage to implement the vision will kill the organization just as the water boiled the frog.

Your style of leadership will need to evolve to meet the situation that you are in. Leadership is tough. Sometimes your subordinates/teammates/children will love you and at other times they will literally hate you for the decisions that you make. As a leader, you must do what you know is morally right and lead. It will be lonely at the top at times but your job is to lead, to provide vision, to provide inspiration, and to ensure the mission is accomplished. At times you will be perceived as the "hard ass" that enforces standards and at other times you will be perceived as the hero that looked out for your people. At other times you will have to go back to your people and state that you made a mistake, you are sorry, and how you will correct the situation.

Situation 11, Rising levels of leadership, style must evolve

Now, as one rises in levels of responsibility, the style of leadership must evolve. What worked when you managed two people is not necessarily a good approach for leading 100 people. One leader can not manage everything and as one's level of leadership increases, one must develop strong subordinates to run the operations as you develop a higher calling (See Chapter 5, Counseling; Chapter 12, Developing Others; and Chapter 13, Delegation of Authority). Before becoming a leader you may have been a technical expert, but now you must orchestrate the big picture by synchronizing operations, HR, and supply in order to do what is best for the overall organization, not the individual departments.

Situation 12, Leadership at home

The leadership aspects listed in this chapter apply to the office, the sports team, and home, but how does one lead at home? The key at home is to be consistent in your values and learn what style is appropriate and when it is appropriate for your family members. Will you blow it? Yes, and you will have to persevere through the failures. Leadership at home is the most challenging of all because you have to live with your family and they know you and how to manipulate you better than anyone.

Keep in mind, the primary leadership style that worked for a child when he was two, will not work when he is eight, and what worked at eight will not work at age fifteen. To complicate matters even more, a primary leadership style that worked for one child won't necessarily work for another child and it usually doesn't.

In conclusion, everyone has a different "natural" leadership style. You have to recognize what style is yours, so you can identify your own strengths and weaknesses and so you know the appropriate times to deviate as the situation calls for it. Being a guider/motivator is great at most times, but if there is an emergency and something has to be done this minute that you know how to do, it is time to move into dictator or micro-manager mode for the task at hand. Don't stay that way for too long or you will burn out your people.

Do you lead by fear? Are you a yeller? Do you do what everyone else wants you to do? Do you never listen to anyone else? Do you micro-manage everything? Do you resist change? Are you complacent in the status quo? Do you require favors for your support? Or do you develop people and motivate them? As you rise in leadership, does your style evolve? Do you know when to change your leadership style?

Note: A leader must always stay consistent in trust and integrity. Once lost, they may not ever be regained.

Chapter 18

The First Report is Always Wrong and Don't Overreact!

Situation 1, Oh no!

"Jack, John lost the compruter with all the employee data on it!" You react by thinking, "Oh, crap, the boss is going to kill me!" I better tell him now. So you tell the boss and the boss asks you a bunch of questions that you don't have the answers to. Now the boss is mad, you feel sick to your stomach, and then 15 minutes later you find out John didn't lose his computer after all!

What really happened is John told Gary he couldn't remember if he left his laptop at home or not and when John called home, Gary overheard John's wife say it is not here. But before you know it, Gary told Tim and Tim told you. What am I getting at? Ninety-five percent of the time the first report is always WRONG! There will be an element of truth to it, but all the facts are not in so don't overreact! Ask some pointed questions and make sure you get updated. Once you have done that, then you can inform your boss what is going on and how you are handling the situation. Your boss will feel more comfortable and so will your subordinates.

One of the most important tasks of a leader is to stay calm in a crisis and think about what needs to be done. If you run around like a chicken with its head cut off, you are now part of the problem and not part of the solution (See Chapter 1 if you need a refresher). It is critical for the leader to step up and take charge in a crisis.

Before reporting to higher about an incident, ask relevant questions and get details. Think of how being informed 20 minutes from now or being informed tomorrow morning with more relevant information affects the situation?

Note: Bad news never gets better with time and if you have to report something the moment you find out, state, "This is an initial report and the facts are not yet confirmed. I am working on finding out the facts now and will update you accordingly."

Situation 2, Broken vase

Jimmy was running and slipped. As he was falling one of his flailing arms hit and broke mom's favorite vase in the living room. Jimmy picked up the pieces and then went to find his mom. Once he found her, Jimmy said in a real apologetic voice, "Mom, I broke your favorite vase that you keep in the living room. I'm sorry."

Mom: "You stupid idiot! I can't believe you did that! I expect that from a 5 year old, but not from you. Go to your room!"

If you were Jimmy, would you want to tell the truth after getting yelled at like that? No. Do you think your subordinates, teammates, and children want to be treated like that? Of course not! If you want people to tell you the truth even when it is bad, then you need to be calm and rational when handling the situation.

Situation 3, Unapproachable boss

"Don't tell the boss, he is going to go ballistic," says one employee. "But someone has to tell the boss," you say. "I'm not going to tell him," says another employee. "Me neither," says someone else. "He ripped my head off the last time I told him bad news. Un-uh, not me." The first employee then says, "Well, Doug, it is up to you. Are you going to tell him or not?"

When your subordinates feel that they can't come to you and tell you about problems because of the way you react, you are no longer a leader! I say again, when your subordinates feel that they can't come to you and tell you about problems because of the way you react, you are no longer a leader! A leader can't fix what he doesn't know about. A leader can't inspire people that he hasn't taken time to learn what motivates them.

Situation 4, Injured star player

> Coach: "Steve broke his leg yesterday and he will be out for the rest of the season."

> Players: "There goes the season!" "We can't win without Steve, he is our best player!" "We might as well not play!"

> Coach: "I know it looks bad and losing Steve is a blow, however, all it means now is we have to work as a team more than ever. And us building our team instead of relying on one player will make us a better team and better players as well. We can do it!"

We have all seen this in the movies and in real life too. Many times the team pulls together and achieves a success that no one thought was possible. The first assumptions by the players were wrong. Had the coach overreacted and given in to the apathy of the team, then the first report would have been proved true.

Situation 5, 9/11 News reporting

Do you remember when 9/11 happened? I was staying at my friend and his wife's home. As I was leaving the house to go to work, my friend's wife said a plane accidentally flew into the World Trade Center (WTC). I looked at it on TV and the news was reporting it as a small commuter plane accidentally hit the WTC. I commented, "Let's hope it was an accident and not a terrorist act," and went to work. As I was driving in and listening to a radio talk show, the second plane ran into the WTC. The talk show hosts couldn't believe we had two accidents. I knew instantly it was terrorists for sure, but for the next half hour or more the news proclaimed it was an accident.

The news was wrong. They only had a few facts and jumped to the wrong conclusion. This happens all the time. Situation 6, Overreaction by a parent

Sister: "Mom, Josh cheated! Make him stop please."

And what should mom do? Yell at Josh to play fair? How often does a parent REACT without getting all the facts? Remember, the first report is almost always wrong (there is an element of truth to it but it is not completely correct). Mom needs to ask, "Josh, what do you have to say?" The answer may surprise you. But by getting the input from both sides, Mom can now make a better educated decision on what needs to happen.

Do you fly into a panic at the first report of something bad? Do you shoot the messenger? Are your employees/players/children afraid to tell you when something goes wrong? Do you overreact without knowing the facts?

Chapter 19

Rest

"If you keep up at this pace, you are going to get burned out." Ever hear those words? Think about them. You must pace yourself.

Situation 1, Car analogy

If you drive a car all the time at 100 MPH, what is going to happen to it (assuming you don't wreck)? You would destroy the engine! An engine can't sustain that rate of speed for the long haul. You have to pace yourself. Our bodies aren't designed to operate seven days a week at 12-20 hrs a day. We need a day to recuperate.

Situation 2, God's rest

"And on the seventh day, God rested." If God, who is all powerful, rested, shouldn't you?

Situation 3, Blind donkey story

Many years ago donkeys were used in the silver mines. After having numerous donkeys getting sick all the time, going blind, and many dying, one animal caretaker decided to stop having all the donkeys work seven days a week. Instead, he decided to have a few work six days a week and on the seventh day, the donkeys would be pulled out of the mines, taken to the surface, and set loose to graze.

After a few months, the caretaker realized that the donkeys that rested one day a week had their stamina return, they didn't get sick, and those with failing vision had their vision return to normal! So, the animals worked less, but produced more! He of course, then made all the animals work a six day work week.

What does that mean to us? We need at least a day a week to relax and clear our mind from the stresses of work. We need to sit back and enjoy life. Forget about work for a day. And for those of us that have a spouse taking care of children, your spouse needs a day without the kids!

While in a combat environment, I developed a plan of how my section could work smarter and not harder. Other sections worked 7 days a week at 16-20 hours a day. I worked my section 10-12 hrs a day and mandated a six day work week. What happened?

Within a few months, the other sections were exhausted, morale was low, and support was not that great. My section, which previously was the most "broke"(poor performing) section in our unit of 2,200 Soldiers was now performing at peak performance, morale was high, and customers loved us! What happened? One key component is that we took time to rest! It does not matter where you are or what you are doing, your mind and body need at least one day of rest a week.

Situation 4, During the day

Throughout the day, take short breaks every hour or so because you can't be at the top of your game all day long. To have "ah-hah!" moments when it all comes together, you need to take 10-15 minute breaks now and then. Walk away from your desk, sit in a relaxing chair, and/or talk to a subordinate.

Are you always going 100 MPH? When was the last time you took a day off and completely refrained from work? When did your spouse last get a day off? Don't be a seven day a week donkey that doesn't know any better! And if you need to take a vacation, schedule one. Remember, all work and no play makes Jack a dull boy.

This chapter is short because I want you to go rest!

Chapter 20

So What?

For today's reading please also include Chapter 21, Work Smarter, Not Harder. These two chapters are very closely related.

In everything you do ask, "So what?" Whether it is preparing a presentation, buying a car, developing a play, or reading a book.

Then, before you take any action, again think, "So what?" Everything you do should answer the so what question. What do you want your action to convey?

Ever heard a question like this before? "John, that was a great presentation and your charts are wonderful, but what is your point?" or "Coach, that was a great speech, but what does that mean to us?"

When you want others to buy into your ideas, they have to understand the "So what?" as it applies to them. Therefore, you must know your audience (See Chapter 11) and present your ideas in such a way that the audience sees the benefit of your idea.

We constantly miss the relevance in our business and personal actions. In all that we do, we should ask the "So what?" question. Why? Doing work for the sake of doing work is a waste of time. That is why by asking "So what?" you see if your actions positively or negatively affect the goal you are trying to achieve. If your actions only add minimal value or none at all, don't do them! If your actions take away from or harm the goal, don't do them! You say no one is that dumb. Well, we do it all the time. For example:

Situation 1, Building materials

Let's say you have a bunch of building materials delivered to a work site. Wouldn't it make more sense to have the supplies delivered to where they are needed instead of just dropping them off at one spot and then having to move them to another spot because now they are in the way? The "So what?" is now you have paid people twice to move your building materials and lost the time that could have been used for building to moving.

Situation 2, Sprinkler system

Outside of my office they built a little park. In the park is a 200 foot area where they ripped out the grass that used to be there, tilled the dirt up, and then replanted the lawn with new grass. A week later after the grass seedlings have already sprouted, then they decide to put a sprinkler system in and had to dig a trench that ruined the perfect grass! The "So what?" is why didn't they put in the sprinkler system before planting the grass saving time, money, and destruction?

Situation 3, Business meeting

John from supply gets up and talks for 10 minutes about how paperclips have increased 25% in cost to $1.25 a package. Then Bart from operations talks for 30 minutes about this great little project he is developing. Then Cary from personnel talks for 20 minutes about problems she is having communicating to legal. And you, you are bored out of your mind and wondering what does this have to do with me? You have wasted an hour of your time already, there are another 8 briefers to go, and little has been accomplished! In fact, instead of being more productive, this meeting has made you less productive!

When you call a meeting, the meeting should have a set end state (the So what?). All briefers talk to that end state. If you have a problem that does not impact the others in the meeting, then this meeting is not the place to bring up your problem.

Situation 4, Workflow management tool

A company was developing a workflow management tool. In the tool, you could schedule someone to one task for a certain amount of time. This tool was great for a production line where people only have one job (task).

The people who developed this tool were all proud of themselves until an employee asked the "So what?" The "So what?" is what if a person was assigned multiple tasks to be performed in a certain amount of time, how do you account for that? The employee was sure the organization this tool was developed for would assign people more than one task at a time.

Well, the developer ignored the employee's concerns and about $200k later the organization the tool was developed for asked the same questions the concerned employee did and then it promptly rejected the product.

If the developer had asked the "So what?" at the beginning of the project or listened to the concerned employee's advice in the early stages and adjusted course, the organization would not have wasted $200k, the developer would have won the $1M contract, and the organization would have gotten the workflow management tool it needed.

Situation 5, "Wet" lubricant versus "dry" lubricant

A certain organization is in charge of weapon lubricants. It has to make a choice concerning a "wet" lubricant and a "dry" lubricant for use in a desert environment. Now, a little education is in order.

A "wet" lubricant is applied "wet" to a weapon and remains "wet" on the weapon. It is this wetting that prevents metal-to-metal friction. The "wet" lubricant is also classified as HAZMAT and is not allowed to be used in enclosed spaces because of the fumes it gives off. It also burns off the weapon in hot temperatures that are a regular occurrence in the desert.

The "wet" lubricant is classified as CLP (Cleaner, Lubricant, and Preservative).

The "dry" lubricant is applied "wet" to the weapon and when heated, bonds to the metal and provides constant lubrication even though it feels dry to the touch. The "dry" lubricant is Non-HAZMAT so it can be used anywhere. It also can be used in any temperature extreme. The "dry" lubricant is classified as XC-DCLP (eXtreme Conditions- Dry, Cleaner, Lubricant, and Preservative).

The "So what?" is that since CLP is a "wet" lubricant, it will always attract sand and dirt, especially in a desert environment. This sand and dirt attraction to wetness will act like a dust magnet on convoys causing weapons to jam when needed most. The rest of the "So what?" is since XC-DCLP is a "dry" lubricant, it will not attract sand and dirt. Thus, weapons' work right the first time, every time, and will not jam in combat. Therefore, troops in the field overwhelmingly say CLP does not work well in the desert and that XC-DCLP does work well in the desert.

So, which one would you choose, the "wet" or the "dry" lubricant? It is a no-brainer- you would choose the "dry" lubricant. Before you make your final decision, though, let's throw a little mud into it.

The "wet" lubricant passed all the lab tests and the "dry" lubricant did not pass all the lab tests (Note: The tests that the dry lubricant failed at the lab, it excelled at in the real world). Now, which lubricant would you choose? Ask yourself the "So what?"

Well, that is not what the organization chose. It chose CLP because CLP passed all the lab tests and XC-DCLP did not pass all the lab tests. The organization missed the "So what?" that mattered, what works in the real world.

Instead of putting thousands of troops at risk and wasting millions of dollars trying to make a "wet" lubricant work in a sandy and dusty environment, if the organization had asked, "So what?," it would have approved the "dry" lubricant and it could have wisely invested the money it used trying to make CLP work elsewhere to the benefit of our troops and the bill payers.

Situation 6, The family vacation

How many times does the father and/or mother make the decision of where to go and what to do for the vacation? The "So what?" is where is the kids' input? If you want the kids to look forward to a family trip and for everyone to have some family quality bonding time, you must include your children's input. The "So what?" if you ignore them is you drive them away form you.

Am I saying do all they want? No, but a day or two out of five doing activities they want or going to certain restaurants or hotels makes a big difference.

Situation 7, Shopping

When I was a little boy, my mother would take me shopping with her. Little boys do not like shopping, at least not this one. My mother needed to shop and no one else could take care of me so she thought, "So what?"

Almost every time we went shopping, my mother made me a deal. If I was good, I would get to go to the toy store or a pet store if we were in a shopping mall. If grocery shopping, I could get a .25 cent toy from the gumball machines or a pack of trading cards from the gas station. The "So what?" for me was if I didn't act right, I lost my privilege and I got a spanking. The "So what?" of the situation was my mother was consistent in the reward and the discipline so very quickly I became a good boy.

Situation 8, Base stealing

You are on third base. There are two outs. There are two strikes and zero balls against the batter. It is the ninth inning and your worst batter is at the plate. The "So what?" is do you try to steal home on the next pitch? Some times you have to balance risks.

Situation 9, Commercialism

Society tells us wee need to celebrate Christmas and Valentine's Day with gifts on those days. Prices leading up to the events are high even with so-called sales to attract people in. Why pay unnecessarily high prices if you don't have to? In my family, we celebrate Christmas (gift giving) after Christmas, we celebrate Valentine's Day a few days after Valentine's Day, and celebrate other events as appropriate. Not only do we get most items at 50% or more off, but we also don't have to wait in lines and fight crowds in restaurants so we enjoy our gifts and meals even more. As for decorations, we buy the decorations after this year's holidays for the next year's holidays at rock bottom prices. Don't buy into commercialism, shop smarter (The "So what?).

Situation 10, Building a house

A new, beautiful looking house was just built not too far from where I live. No expense was spared and the home was perfectly situated so the bedrooms would receive the rising sun and the dining room would be bathed in the setting sun. Wonderful, right? Well, the builders forgot to ask, "So what?" when deciding where to place the house on the lot. You see, they put the garage door on the side of the house where there was only ten feet of property between the house and the property line leaving no turning radius to get into the garage or out of the garage with a vehicle!

Now, the home will sell for a much lower price than it would have commanded. The home buyer will have to remove the original garage door and replace it with brick. Then, he will have to knock out part of the wall in the front of the house to install the garage door there along with having to install a new driveway if he wants to garage his car. Had the builder placed the house in a more favorable position on the property, say twenty feet from the property line (there was plenty of room), the problem would have been avoided in the first place.

In everything you do, you need to ask the "So what?" When presenting an idea to someone, will he understand the "So what?" you want to convey? When you have a meeting, what is the "So what?" or are you just wasting time? When you make a decision about a product, did you answer the "So what?" that really matters? When making decisions that affect others, did you consider their "So what?" input? When making any decision, have you asked, "What are the "So what?" results of your decision down to the second and third order effects?"

Chapter 21

Work Smarter, Not Harder

Working harder not smarter is unfortunately what most of us do and it takes many forms. Some places you have to be at work until 5 PM even though you finished the task at 3 PM.

If I have seen this once, I have seen it a thousand times! Working harder not smarter is unfortunately what most of us do and it takes many forms. In everything you do, think, "Does this make sense? Is there a better way of doing this?" Don't just start working and not question. Only a fool builds a house without a plan.

Situation 1, Assembly line

If you are running an assembly line, does it make more sense to have C in front of A instead of after B? If C is the limiting factor it might. Work smarter, not harder!

Situation 2, Canoeing

When paddling a canoe, if both paddlers paddle in unison on opposite sides, then the canoe will go straight and move faster with less effort than if both paddlers paddle at different times or on the same side. Work smarter, not harder!

Situation 3, Overloaded

How many times have you seen a person trying to balance working five or ten tasks? Usually, what you see is most of them being performed under standard or always being finished late. Maybe the person should prioritize the tasks, work on one to three tasks, and delegate the rest out. Bet you would find that productivity increased, morale increased, and all you did was redistribute the work. Work smarter, not harder!

Situation 4, Frozen bolt

How many of you have tried to unloosen a bolt and the wrench wouldn't budge it? And you continued to try and turn (push) that wrench with all your might until it moved? Wouldn't it be smarter to put some penetrating oil on the bolt and put an extension tube over the wrench handle so you have more leverage and have to use less strength to turn the wrench? Yes, work smarter, not harder!

Situation 5, Shopping

What if you make a list of things you need to get and then group the stores that are near each other and go by one set of stores one day and the other group the next? You will save time, gas, and frustration along with freeing up time to do other things. Shop smarter, not harder ☺. For me, I always take the car that needs the most gas to church on Sunday, because the gas station with the best prices is located on the way to church. Therefore, I am not making an extra trip to get gas, I get a better price, and I feel happier.

Situation 6, Homework

Let's say you don't understand a problem. Do you just spend all your time being frustrated and trying to do that one problem or do you try and solve the other problems first? Solve the other problems you know how to do first. It will build your confidence, it may trigger an idea, and then you can go back to the problem you are stuck on. Worst case scenario is you get everything else finished, except what you did not understand. Work smarter, not harder!

Situation 7, Vacuuming

If you vacuum with a vacuum cleaner that doesn't clean, whether you vacuum one time or 1,000 times, it still won't clean. Do you still vacuum? Ok, don't answer that question. The answer should be, "no" and then go get a vacuum that cleans! Work smarter, not harder!

Situation 8, Reports

You have two departments that need to gather information in your organization. Unfortunately, they don't talk to each other so they each send you a separate template and different suspense dates. Therefore, you get asked to fill out the information twice in two different formats! It is a waste of both your time and the two departments. Had the two departments coordinated their actions, there would be one easy format, one report to update, and more time for everyone to do other tasks! Work smarter, not harder!

Situation 9, Meetings

Let's say you have a staff meeting every Monday morning, but the information you need to brief won't be complete until Monday night. By having the meeting on Monday morning, you now have to gather data over the weekend and it still will not be fully accurate. You will also still have to get updates at the end of the day. Why not have the meeting Tuesday morning instead, not work on Sunday, and have the correct information the first time? Work smarter, not harder!

Situation 10, Racquetball

In racquetball, the experienced person that places their shot well does not have to move around (run) much. By you placing the shot well, the other player, on the other hand, has to run all over the place in order to hit the ball. The experienced player thus works smarter, not harder!

Situation 11, Exercise

You want to exercise and you want to watch TV, but you don't have time to do both separately. Watch the TV while exercising. Work smarter, not harder!

Situation 12, Coaching

Your team needs to work on physical conditioning and basketball control in addition to other tasks, but you don't have time to do them all. Combine the most important tasks. For example, have players run sprints in one direction and on the return sprint, have them sprint as fast as they can while dribbling the ball.

Situation 13, Kids in the house.

You need to talk to your kids. One child is upstairs, the other is in the basement, and you are downstairs. Instead of yelling to each one of them and going back and forth and getting frustrated because you don't hear each other well, call one to you, explain to the one to get the other sibling, and then with them next to you, speak to them both. Save your lungs and frustration, work smarter, not harder!

Situation 14, Tools.

Use the right tool for the right job. A screwdriver does not take the place of a hammer and vice-versa. Likewise, don't send a sales clerk to do the manager's job. The list is endless. Using the wrong tool generally causes more problems than the problem you are trying to correct in the first place.

Are you working harder or smarter? Stop and think! What do your employees/family/players think? What are their suggestions? Is there a better way of doing things? Are you working to standard or to time? Working smarter not harder is closely related to "Chapter 20, So What?"

Chapter 22

Effective Listening

Situation 1, One sided conversation

Wife: "Mike, we need to get…."

Husband: Eyes fixated on the computer responds, "Yep, I got it."

Wife: Continues to tell instructions.

Husband: Continues to work at the computer while occasionally saying, "Got it."

Wife: Asks, "Are you listening to me?

Husband: "Yeah."

Wife: "Repeat what I just asked you to do."

Husband: Stops working at the computer, faces wife, and says, "Say what?"

Wife: "I'm serious, repeat what I just asked you to do."

Husband: "Ok, you want…" (misses half the stuff)

Wife: "You forgot this…."

Mike wasn't really listening to his wife, he was focusing on the computer. How often is one person doing something else and not paying attention to the person that is talking? That is not effective communication. To have effective communication, you must have effective listening.

Effective listening is critical to establishing successful communication. It is a very important skill every leader must develop. Without it, information literally goes in one ear and out the other, the person who is trying to communicate with you gets frustrated, and you get frustrated.

There are many great books on the subject of effective listening that go into great detail, so I will not try to copy them but give you some general advice for effective listening.

1. Have eye-to-eye contact with the person you are talking to and eliminate all distracters (Looking at the computer, watching TV, etc.). Even if someone hears what you said, if they are not looking at you, they miss out on a lot of your body language which usually conveys even more than your words.
2. Have the person restate back to you what you said by saying words to the effect, "I understand you said _____,_____,_____ and you meant _____,_____,_____."
3. If the person does not restate properly, repeat steps 1-2.
4. When speaking or listening, look at non-verbal clues. If someone is scowling, rolling their eyes, playing with their nails, etc., that person is not really listening.
5. When listening, don't think ahead completing the other person's thought or think about other things. Give the person speaking your undivided attention.

Yes, I know these five steps are truly tough, especially taking the time to do steps 1-3 and step 5, however, it will transform your communication. Try it. You will be amazed at how much miscommunication you have that you were previously unaware of.

Situation 2, Effective listening, your body

Effective listening is not just a skill you do with others. It is something you need to do with yourself also. Too often we ignore our bodies until we are sick or in pain. But there is something good that can come out of pain.

If you listen to your inner voice, you can hear what is important to you and what is not. For example, if you are sick and in pain and you are crying out to God, "I will give up this and that if you make me feel better," that is your conscience speaking to you that you need to take better care of yourself. If you are thinking, "I don't spend enough time with my kids," you are not.

In either case God does not make deals (bargain), however, listen to your body so you will not injure it and listen to your conscience so you can do what is right. Your body and conscience will thank you for it.

Situation 3, Email

Boss: "Brian, how come you didn't do _____?

Brian: "What are you talking about? You never told me about it."

Boss: Angrily says, "I sent it in an email to you two days ago."

Brian: "I didn't get the email Sir."

Whenever you have something important that must be done, don't just send an email, call! When I was an operations officer and I needed something from my subordinate units ASAP, I would email the information and then have a secretary call the subordinate units telling the units to check the email and call me immediately if they had any questions or did not get the email.

Fire and forget emails are not effective communication! They are a recipe for disaster and are examples of poor leadership in action.

Situation 4, You and the kid

> Mom: "Are you listening to me?"

> Jackie: In front of the TV, "Yeah, Mom."

> Mom: "What did I just tell you?"

> Jackie: "Well, you wanted me to...."

> Mom: "Jackie, turn off the TV and then look at me so I make this clear."

> Jackie: "Mom!"

> Mom: "Don't "Mom" me. Lose the attitude (Jackie is pouting)." "That's better. I need you to take out the trash and clean the living room, then you can watch TV."

> Jackie: "But, Mom…" and seeing Mom's face stops.

> Mom: "What needs to happen?"

> Jackie: "I need to take out the trash and then clean the living room before I can watch TV."

> Mom: "Thank you."

Mom had to get rid of the TV distraction and then the attitude that cropped up in Jackie so they could effectively communicate. By being able to see Mom's body language, Jackie knew Mom was serious and began to listen.

Situation 5, The coach and the team

> Coach: "Stop! What are you boys doing?"

> Players: "We are just executing the play you told us to Coach."

Coach: "Are you kidding me? You didn't even come close to the play. John, what are you supposed to do?

John: "Go to the far post."

Coach: "Good. Bob?"

Bob: "That means I am supposed to go to the near post then Coach."

Coach: "Yes, that is correct. Josh how about you?"

Josh: "Go to the top of the key Coach."

Coach: "Good. Mike?"

Mike: "If I don't have the ball. Go to the strong side."

Coach: "Thank you Mike. Dave?"

Dave: "Coach I thought you said I was to go to the strong side, not the weak side."

Coach: "Mike, you need to get your head in the game. I need you. A mistake like that can cost us the game. You are to break toward the weak side when you have the ball. Now let me know you understand."

Dave: "Break to the weak side if I have the ball, strong if I don't."

Coach: "Good, let's run it again until we have it down pat."

Do you listen to others or are you thinking about something else while they are talking? Do you restate back to others what you think you heard and seek clarification? Do you give others your undivided attention? Do your employees/ teammates/family think you listen well (remember, their perception is reality, See Chapter 7, Do as I Say, Not as I Do if you need a refresher)? Do you send fire and forget emails? Are other people listening to you? Are you reading their non-verbal cues? If it doesn't seem like they are listening, do you ask them to restate what you just said?

Chapter 23

Don't Write Checks You Can't Honor

Situation 1, Promises can't keep

"John, I am telling you, keep working hard, you are going to get a $5,000 raise."

"Thanks Keith"

Two months later the new salaries come out and there was no raise. Keith didn't have the authority to give a raise. Keith also had no idea what, if any, raises were going to be handed out. How do you think morale is now after being promised something and given nothing? Is this a quick fix? No!

Situation 2, Promise a little, do more

Junior Manager: "Sir, I don't know if I can do all that, but I can promise you I can do A and B."

Senior Manager: "Jim, I really need C done."

Junior Manager: "Sir, I am confident I can get A and B done, but I am not sure I can get C done. I want to give you a quality product."

Junior Manager: Two days later. "Sir, I was able to get A, B, C, and D complete."

Senior Manager: "Jim, that is more than I expected! This is tremendous. I know I can always count on you."

Had Jim only been able to do A and B, his boss would have been satisfied. But being able to do C and D, the boss was overjoyed. Had Jim promised to do C, but only had the time to perform A and B, then Jim would have angered his boss. Commit to what you know you can do. Don't promise what you can't deliver; it will come back to bite you sooner than you know.

Situation 3, Rewards

> Dad: "Son, if you get all A's on your report card, I will buy you a dog."
>
> Son: "Do you promise Dad?"
>
> Dad: "Yes, son."

Johnny brings home all A's on his report card and you don't get him a dog for whatever reason (You can't afford it, you don't want it, you didn't think your son would get all A's, it doesn't matter). How do you think your son feels? "Oh, he will get over it," you say. No, he won't and his motivation to excel has just been severely decreased. Why should he trust you, you never got him the pet he wanted to love and take care of. Never make a promise you don't intend to or can't keep.

Situation 4, Win the championship

> Coach: "Kids, if you stay focused during practice and we win the championship, I will take you all out for pizza."

The kids win the championship and the coach doesn't take them out for pizza. What do they remember about you? "I can't believe Coach lied to us." "He is so cheap." "I can't believe Coach let us down."

Your status as a positive role model crashed. How will the kids trust you now? If you make a promise, you must keep it. If you can not keep a promise, you have to admit your failure and provide an alternative.

Are you writing checks you can't honor? Are you making flippant promises you can't keep? Do you realize you are destroying the morale of your employees/family/and players?

Think about it. Every time you write a check you can't keep, your credibility decreases. Is that what you want?

Chapter 24

Self Discipline

Situation 1, Pride

       I never wanted a tattoo in my life, but when I was 19 I got one. You see, I was working on pools this day and it was raining like cats and dogs. It was miserable outside, but I was a macho man and the guy I was working with had a cool eagle tattoo on his forearm. Well, we got to talking and then he challenged my manhood and in so many words I would be a wimp if I did not get a tattoo. Now, I was physically fit, full of testosterone, and my mind shut down. I couldn't let him think I was a wimp! And even though I never wanted a tattoo, I let pride get in the way and I got one.

       Pride is at the root of giving into all negative peer pressure. Think about it! You wouldn't do that stupid thing if you weren't seeking approval or cared about what other people think. You are afraid of losing face, so your pride says, "Do it" even if your mind says, "No." So, pride = negative peer pressure and we all are susceptible to it (Not just kids, but adults are susceptible on a daily basis too). Negative peer pressure is when we let pride in the way. We care more about what other people think than what really matters. Pride makes us do dumb things.

       Well, what does pride have to do with self discipline? Everything! A leader that lets pride get in the way of making good decisions for the organization puts the organization into turmoil. The bible states that pride brings destruction. Leaders, therefore, must humble themselves and look at the big picture. The leader has to admit when he is wrong and he then has to come on line and support the better plan of action. Your employees will admire you for coming to your senses. Your boss may or may not approve, but in my experience, my bosses looked at me as being invaluable because I would do what is right.

Situation 2, Setting time aside

Why is it some people are strong and some people are overweight? Most people that are strong set aside time to exercise on a regular basis. Most people that are overweight don't follow an exercise schedule and eat in an undisciplined manner (anytime).

Why are some people knowledgeable and others aren't? For the most part, knowledgeable people set aside time to study on a regular basis and the unlearned do not.

You must schedule time for yourself to develop yourself physically and mentally. "Well, I don't have enough time to do it all," you say and you are right. You must prioritize what things are important. You may need to wake up thirty minutes earlier to eat breakfast. Instead of listening to the radio in the morning, listen to a motivational speaker or a language tape. Maybe you waste three hours in front of the TV doing nothing. Instead, watch a movie only when you exercise and kill two birds with one stone.

Self discipline is a habit you choose to create and follow! Now, a habit takes approximately 28 days/times to build. There are many tools that can help you build and follow the self discipline habit.

Mark your calendar with the scheduled event you need to perform and review your calendar daily.

Have someone encourage you daily to discipline yourself.

If you have a temptation problem, remove the temptation and replace the temptation with a safe substitute item or activity. It will be tough, but you can do it.

I have never seen a great leader that did not posses a great deal of self discipline. Self discipline truly separates the dreamers from the achievers.

Situation 3, Practice makes perfect

What makes great athletes great? Well, they may have some natural talent, but what really sets them apart from the average person is practice.

Michael Jordan and Larry Bird spent hours practicing free throws and other drills on their own time. Tiger Woods began practicing golf when he was a boy and the list goes on and on. The simple truth is the professionals make the tough look easy only because they practice to be perfect.

Situation 4, Managing finances

This seems to be an epidemic problem in the U.S. Managing finances is possible for anyone if you exercise self discipline and you create a simple plan to follow. I follow the 20/80 rule. Ten percent of my pay goes directly to my church and then 10% goes directly to my savings plan. The other 80% goes to paying the bills in the charts below. Chart 1 is a weekly and monthly money tracking chart and Chart 2 is a monthly tracking chart. I have used both charts and now that I am pretty disciplined, I am using Chart 2 instead of Chart 1. Both are good.

To use Chart 1, once a week or daily update the appropriate weekly column with amounts spent.

To use Chart 2, once a week or daily update the monthly column with amounts spent.

Chart 1, Weekly and Monthly Finance Chart Combined

Category	September Monthly Goal %	Monthly Goal Amount	Actual Spent %	Actual Spent Amount
Tithe	10.00%	360	10.00%	360
Investing	10.00%	360	10.00%	360
House Payment	22.22%	800	22.22%	800
Car Payment	8.06%	290	8.06%	290
Car Parts	4.17%	150	1.39%	50
Car & Home Insure	5.56%	200	5.56%	200
Medical Insurance	16.67%	600	16.67%	600
Telephone Bill	2.22%	80	1.86%	67
Power Bill	2.78%	100	3.06%	110
Trash Bill	0.83%	30	0.83%	30
Gas- Car	4.17%	150	3.83%	138
Groceries	5.56%	200	2.78%	100
Dry Cleaning	0.83%	30	1.06%	38
Work, Miscellaneous	0.83%	30	0.83%	30
Housing Expenses	1.11%	40	0.69%	25
Entertainment	1.39%	50	2.64%	95
Gifts- Loved ones	2.22%	80	1.25%	45
Other	1.39%	50	2.39%	86
	100.00%	$3,600	95.11%	$3,424

Monthly percentage and dollar amount PLAN to spend

Monthly percentage and dollar amount ACTUALLY spent

| | Week 1 | | Week 2 | | Week 3 | | Week 4 |
| | Sep 1-7 | | Sep 8-15 | | Sep 16-23 | | Sep 24-31 |
%	Amount	%	Amount	%	Amount	%	Amount
6.67%	240	0.00%		3.33%	120	0.00%	
3.33%	120	0.00%		6.67%	240	0.00%	
0.00%		22.22%	800	0.00%		0.00%	
8.06%	290	0.00%		0.00%		0.00%	
0.83%	30	0.00%		0.00%		0.56%	20
2.78%	100	1.39%	50	1.39%	50	0.00%	
16.67%	600	0.00%		0.00%		0.00%	
0.00%		0.00%		0.00%		1.86%	67
0.00%		3.06%	110	0.00%		0.00%	
0.00%		0.83%	30	0.00%		0.00%	
0.61%	22	1.00%	36	1.06%	38	1.17%	42
0.56%	20	0.00%		1.11%	40	1.11%	40
0.00%		0.33%	12	0.44%	16	0.28%	10
0.42%	15	0.00%		0.00%		0.42%	15
0.42%	15	0.00%		0.00%		0.28%	10
0.00%		1.11%	40	1.53%	55	0.00%	
0.00%		1.25%	45	0.00%		0.00%	
0.00%		1.39%	50	0.00%		1.00%	36
	$1,452	40.33%	$1,173	32.58%	$559	15.53%	$240

Weekly total
dollar
amount
ACTUALLY
spent

Percent of
total budget
ACTUALLY
spent this
week

Chart 2, Monthly Finance Chart

HOUSING	Goal	Actual	Difference	Percent	Actual %
Mortgage	$1,500	$0	$1,500	30%	0%
Insurance	$120	$0	$120	2%	0%
Water	$30	$0	$30	1%	0%
Electric	$80	$0	$80	2%	0%
Telephone	$80	$0	$80	2%	0%
Repair	$50	$0	$50	1%	0%
Subtotals	$1,860	$0	$1,860	37%	0%
TRANSPORTATION	Goal	Actual	Difference	Percent	Actual %
Insurance- car	$80	$0	$80	2%	0%
Fuel	$150	$0	$150	3%	0%
Maintenance	$50	$0	$50	1%	0%
Subtotals	$280	$0	$280	6%	0%
Health	Goal	Actual	Difference	Percent	Actual %
Health insurance	$585	$0	$585	12%	0%
Subtotals	$585	$0	$585	12%	0%
FOOD	Goal	Actual	Difference	Percent	Actual %
Groceries	$330	$0	$330	7%	0%
Dining out	$150	$0	$150	3%	0%
Subtotals	$480	$0	$480	10%	0%
Family and pet	Goal	Actual	Difference	Percent	Actual %
Dog food	$25	$0	$25	1%	0%
Dog-flea, tick, med	$30	$0	$30	1%	0%
Child allowance	$40	$0	$40	1%	0%
Subtotals	$95	$0	$95	2%	0%
ENTERTAINMENT	Goal	Actual	Difference	Percent	Actual %
Trips	$100	$0	$100	2%	0%
Other- Gifts, etc	$50	$0	$50	1%	0%
Subtotals	$150	$0	$150	3%	0%
SAVINGS	Goal	Actual	Difference	Percent	Actual %
Retirement account	$500	$0	$500	10%	0%
Other	$500	$0	$500	10%	0%
Subtotals	$1,000	$0	$1,000	20%	0%
DONATIONS	Goal	Actual	Difference	Percent	Actual %
Church	$500	$0	$500	10%	0%
Other	$50	$0	$50	1%	0%
Subtotals	$550	$0	$550	11%	0%
Grand total	$5,000	$0	($5,000)	100%	0%

Note: The monthly Finance Chart was derived from a Microsoft Excel file I had previously seen.

When I get a pay raise, I immediately add 10% to the church, 10% to savings, 50% of it goes to investing/ paying down extra principal on the mortgage, and the other 30% is left over for whatever.

Most people blow the raise they get on new toys and create more debt for themselves. Don't fall into that trap! Pay down your bills instead!

And when it comes to credit cards, if you can't pay if off at the end of the month, don't purchase the item! It is better to only have a little and be able to sleep at night because you can pay your bills, then to have a lot of things and wonder how you are going to pay for it all during your restless nights.

Practice some self discipline. You can do it.

Note: A leader that can not manage his finances, will not be a leader for long.

Situation 5, Good grades

Steve: "How did you do on your test?"

Dave: "I got a D. My dad is going to kill me."

Steve: "Did you study?"

Dave: "No, I was playing the new Nintendo game. It was awesome! So, how did you do on the test?"

Steve: "I got an A."

Dave: "You studied, didn't you?"

Steve: "Sure did. I am going to go to college on a scholarship and my dad said he would give me half the money he saved due to the scholarship, when I graduate."

Now, homework can be studying for school, preparing for a presentation, reading directions before putting something together, and so on. The key thing is practice before you do the real thing.

Note: In the example above, Dave has tunnel vision (caught in the here and now) and Steve sees the big picture (his future).

Situation 6, Exercise

Getting into an exercise routine is tough for most of us. The way I do it is I get up early in the morning three times a week, drink a glass of water, and then I go down stairs. I turn on the TV and pop a DVD into the DVD player, stretch, and then workout.

When I work out is when I watch movies so it is like tying in a reward to motivate me. Some people will need a partner to help encourage. Whatever you do, if you tie in a small reward, it will help encourage your good behavior.

Are there times when I still don't want to exercise? Yes! Do I skip? Almost never. I find that I feel so much better about myself when I exercise regularly compared to when I don't. I also like to eat, so by exercising regularly, I can eat more of what I want ☺.

Before I started exercising regularly at the age of 15, I was a 90 lb weakling. I went up to almost 180 lbs of muscle at my peak and now I settle at 160 lbs. If I can do it, you can do it. What sets apart a dreamer from an achiever is self discipline.

Situation 7, Self evaluation- Mountains

When my wife and I were in Costa Rica on our honeymoon (I have gotten married since I wrote Chapter 7 ☺), there was this volcano we could see from our hotel. Most of the time the volcano was covered in clouds and all you could see was the base of the volcano or nothing at all. Occasionally, you could briefly see the volcano through breaks in the clouds. And fortunately for us, we saw it clearly a few times at night when it was erupting.

Are there any mountains in your life? Is there something that is blocking your relationship with God, your loved ones, your co-workers, or your teammates that you don't notice? Just like clouds can hide a mountain, living in a sinful and/or an unhealthy lifestyle will dull our senses to what is wrong and very soon, we don't see our sin or our shortfalls and we become hypocritical, unfruitful people.

There is only one way to rid oneself of the mountain. In the spiritual sense, we must open our eyes to see the mountain, call a sin a sin, confess our sin to God, and turn away from our sin. In the physical sense, we must call a spade a spade, identify the problem and fix it (Chapter 2).

What if it is our family members/friends/teammates/co-workers/or bosses that can't see the mountain? Good question. I think the biblical answer applies to all.

If the other person is clouded in sin or some other fault, we must first examine ourselves (clean our own mess) and then in brotherly love, I say again, in brotherly love confront this person in private. If the person does not listen, confront in front of two or three witnesses. If the person won't listen then, they are a fool and you have done your duty. The issue, if serious, then needs to be brought public.

If you confront the person in public first, before you have done in private, is the person going to think you care about him? Absolutely not. Have I ever made this mistake? Yes, sad to say, even when I knew better. Then, I had to apologize to the person and everyone else that was involved.

Does pride get in the way of your decision making? Are you too good to listen to anyone else? Do you set aside time for yourself? Do you exercise your mind? Do you exercise your body? Do you know your weaknesses? Have you done your homework before taking the real world or school test? Are there mountains in your life that you don't see, because you have clouds in front of them? Have you asked those that are close to you if you have any mountains?

Chapter 25

Setting Others Up for Success

Situation 1, Gone on vacation- Set up for failure

You are left in charge while your boss is on vacation for a few days. Your boss' boss calls down needing a report you never heard of. One of the associates asks you what are we doing on this major issue for which the answer is due today and you don't have a clue of what you should do since you have never heard of this issue before now. Congratulations, you have been set up for failure.

Situation 2, Going on vacation- Setting up for success

Before you go on vacation, you need to set your subordinates up for success. Check with your bosses to see if there are any new requirements that will need to be completed while you are away. Then, review your calendar and make a list of all the requirements that must be met in your absence and assign people to the tasks.

Get with your subordinates and communicate effectively what is required of them (See Chapter 13, Delegation of Authority and Chapter 22, Effective Listening). Things to include are: meetings they must attend, how to act, what to say, what not to say, what resources they can use, when reports are due out, when reports are due, etc.

Also, let your subordinates know where they have authority to make decisions if an issue arises and areas where they must first contact you or your boss before making a decision. If you have time or it is applicable, train your subordinates up prior in the tasks they must perform so the first time they perform the task(s), it is not in your absence. Once they have back briefed you on their responsibilities, then you can see your boss to back brief him on who will be in charge/who to contact and give him a list of this information.

Now, your subordinates are set up for success, your boss is set up for success, and you are set up for success.

Situation 3, Children

I don't give my daughter money. She has to do chores and achieve good grades in school to earn money. With the money she has earned, she has to give 10% of it the church (like I do) and whatsoever she chooses to put into savings, I double. From there, however she spends her money is her choice as long as it is a morally acceptable choice. And when my daughter recently earned a raise in her allowance, my daughter chose to put it all in savings to double her money.

We all want our children to grow up to be respectable, successful people. In order to do that, we must set them up for success. They learn by watching you. We must teach them about respect, modesty, self discipline, and money management. If we don't take the time to teach them and live by example, most likely they will learn all the wrong answers from their friends.

For example, if you don't treat your spouse with respect, do you think your kids will? If you treat the waiter with disrespect, don't you think your kids will follow your lead? If you don't pay your bills, do you think your kids will pay theirs?

Situation 4, Sports

To set a team up for success, the team must learn the basics. Once the team has mastered the basics, then you can start developing the teams' advanced skills. For example, you have to know how to dribble a basketball while walking before trying to dribble while running. Furthermore, if you have practiced a play one way, the coach should not modify the play just before game time without any practice. That is asking for failure if you do.

Situation 5, Taskings

As the operations officer in my organization with six subordinate units, I was responsible for tasking our six subordinate units to perform missions. The taskings could involve personnel, equipment, and/or supplies.

Before I tasked any/some/or all the subordinate units, I would look at the training schedule (calendar of events the units are scheduled to perform) along with other taskings I might have the units performing in addition to the training schedule. I did this so as to balance the taskings proportionally and not cripple any one part of the organization.

Whenever one of the subordinate units questioned my taskings, I sat down with the commander of that unit and showed him how I balanced out the taskings. Out of over two thousand taskings, I only had about ten sit downs with commanders and only needed to make two changes. The two changes came about due to training events that were not on the training calendar. Had I not balanced out the taskings, there would have been many, many more changes.

Situation 6, Report templates

When I was the personnel officer for a 2,000+ person organization, I was responsible for preparing awards for everyone that deserved one. This is tougher than it sounds. I had nine different subordinate organizations that had to submit their deserving people for one of two different types of awards.

One award, we will call it the merit award, included a one page narrative that included personal achievements and an award citation along with an award form that had personal and unit information on it. The other award, we will call it the commendation award, had an award form that had personal and unit information along with personal achievements and an award citation.

To make matters worse, the previous personnel officer just a few months ago had failed miserably when having had to do this for just a few hundred personnel. Deserving peoples' awards were lost or late and I had to resubmit/recreate these awards. I was determined not to let this fiasco happen again.

So, to set my submitting organizations and their personnel up for success and to set myself up for success I created a five step plan.

Step 1: User manual, standardization, and templates

First of all, I created an easy to read idiot-proof, user-friendly manual stating step-by-step how to create each type of award. In the manual, there was an example award template filled out properly and numbered to correspond to the step-by-step instructions for each type of award.

Note: I used the counsel of 2 or 3 people (See Chapter 14, Counsel of 2 or 3) not associated with my area to check to ensure readability and common sense in the manual and the awards.

Secondly, I standardized as much information as legally possible on each of the awards so there would be less chances of errors, to reduce repetitive work, and to decrease the amount of time needed to process each award.

For the commendation award, I created a standard citation and personal achievements that greatly simplified the process. This may seem impersonal, but when dealing with 1,600+ of these types of awards, it would save thousands of hours of time and most importantly, all people would receive their awards in a timely manner.

For the merit award, I created "sample" formats of previously approved narrations for each category of job we had so the preparer would know how to properly write their people up for the merit award.

Finally, I created an electronic version of the award templates for each of the nine organizations with all of the standardized information input into the template already so all the organizations had to do was type in the personnel names, administrative data, and previous awards. This was critical for two reasons. Reason one is everyone had to use the award template I created which ensured my computer system could read their information, thus reducing retyping of unreadable awards by the submitting unit. Reason two is now all my section needed to check on in the submitted awards was the personnel information, thus streamlining our process and significantly decreasing our processing time.

Step 2: Meeting

After I prepared my Step 1 items, I held a meeting with all the personnel chiefs and their lead workers. The lead workers were required to be present because I wanted to ensure there was no miscommunication between the personnel chiefs and the workers. At the meeting, I handed out a copy of the manual, the electronic templates, and a copy of my presentation slides.

After I went through each award format and confirmed from each lead worker that they understood, then I discussed the timeline to turn in the awards, which was a key factor in our success.

Step 3: Staggered turn-in

I created a staggered award turn-in date for all the units (See Chapter 21, Work Smarter, Not Harder). The bigger units of course had more award turn-in dates as they had more awards to process. The staggered turn-in date plan had four key points.

Point 1, the staggered turn-in kept a steady turn-in flow for my office so we could handle the work load and not get back logged.

Point 2, the staggered turn-in gave the subordinate units a reasonable amount of time to get their awards in and because of the staggered turn-ins, they could batch process awards. For example, the first 200 names in alphabetical order were due by turn-in date one, the next 200 by turn-in date two, and so on.

Point 3, by having the staggered turn-in dates before our actual awards' period ended meant that all the units began preparing the awards immediately. This was unheard of, but genius. You see, now all the organizations had a more manageable workload they could handle everyday and not be overwhelmed at the end which would lead to lots of errors. You say, but what if a person doesn't deserve the award? Easy. If the person doesn't deserve the award, we would just tear it up. It is much easier to destroy one or two awards than to try to create thousands of awards at once.

Point 4, the staggered turn-in enabled me to send a steady, manageable flow of awards to my boss on a daily basis so he was not overburdened by signing awards and could also concentrate on his other daily tasks.

Step 4: Updates

I conducted weekly two-minute updates to the leaders of my organization and the subordinate organization leaders to keep them up to date on our progress and if any command influence was needed to correct any substandard performance. I would also periodically visit the subordinate organizations and ask if they had any questions and to check on them.

Step 5: Award orders

I began ordering the actual awards in small batches at the beginning of the nine month award period. By doing so, I had all 2,000+ awards when it was time to present. The ten other like organizations at my level did not and were short awards. I took care of my people by seeing the big picture and ordering early.

The result of the five step plan was that we were the first and only organization to have all their awards complete on time. Every person was recognized appropriately and in a timely manner. Morale was high.

None of this would have happened, however, if I did not set up my subordinate units for success. If you need something from someone, awards in this case, you have to help them help you by doing as much work as you can so they don't have to. That is not my job you say. Wrong! Think big picture, not tunnel vision. By helping them, you help yourself and everyone wins.

So, to set yourself up for success in reports others owe you, follow this checklist.

	Create a template and fill in non-changing information.
	Create step-by-step instructions: Have someone try to follow your instructions to see if your instructions are idiot-proof. Include examples of what right looks like in your instructions.
	Hold a class: Educate users on responsibilities due to you and why.
	Notify others when report is due way in advance, the day prior, and immediately when past due.
	Meetings: Don't drop a dime on those who did not turn in information at the meeting. It creates lasting adversity. Confront person afterwards.

Situation 7, Letter of support

In one company I have worked with, we needed to get a letter of support from a senior leader in government to help fix a situation where another government organization needed a little external pressure to push it to do the right thing.

While technically it is the job of the senior leader's staff to create the letter, don't go that route. If you go that route, it will: take forever, not say what you want it to say, and did I say take forever if it even gets done? The staffer is too busy with other issues just to focus on this. To set the staffer up for success and the organization up for success, I created a draft letter for the staffer that he could edit as needed. Instead of waiting months for the letter if the staffer created it, by me drafting it, the senior leader signed the letter in a few days!

Are you setting other people up for success? Are you setting your subordinates up for success? Are you setting yourself up for success? Have you created checklists to prevent errors? Have you briefed and trained up your subordinates to act in your absence? Are you caught up in the "it's not my job" nonsense? If so, stop, because If you want people to help you, you must help them first. Not only will people be more receptive to your request, but in the future, it makes your working relationship much more pleasant also.

Chapter 26

Advice Across the Spectrum

Plan for the worst, hope for the best in all you do. This way you won't be under resourced or disappointed, but you can be pleasantly surprised.

Work yourself out of a job. This makes you promotable and it develops your people. Everyone wins and you become even more valuable.

A good 80% solution that is timely and everyone understands is better than a 90-100% solution that is late and/or not everyone understands. Perfection is nice, but most plans do not need to be perfect to understand the goal that needs to be achieved. Add in a constantly changing work environment, the perfect product will not be perfect for long.

Trust and respect. As a leader, these must be your cornerstone. If your people do not trust you, they will not respect you. If your people do not respect you, they will not listen (and/or when they have the first opportunity to not listen, then they will disobey).

Don't make a mountain out of a mole-hill. Think before you act, don't blow minor problems out of proportion. How many times do people get angry at something that doesn't matter and then that turns people off and builds resentment? If you attack all the mole-hills, then when there is a mountain, it falls on deaf ears.

If it happens once, shame on me. If it happens twice, shame on you. It is one thing for someone to make a mistake once or pool the wool over your eyes once, but once it has been brought to attention and corrected, if it happens again, then there is a problem.

When in a hole, stop digging! A very wise man taught me this. Whatever the problem is- finances, a lie, the wrong word spoken- STOP! Do not continue to dig the hole by continuing to spend money you don't have, lying more, or saying more stupid things. STOP the madness. If you keep digging, the problem only gets worse, and it gets harder and harder to see daylight. A little hole is much easier to get out of than a well. Own up to your mistake, identify the problem and the solution and work to it. Daylight will come around.

You catch more bees with honey than with vinegar. Or as the bible says, soft words turn away wrath, but grievous words stir up anger. It is hard to win over people when you are insulting them and making them feel stupid. Most people when insulted will dig in and not listen to reason even if they are wrong. Find a way to show them a better solution without insulting. Find some common ground and then offer the solution.

No Whining/Don't criticize. Criticism is complaining without providing a viable solution. Instead of criticizing and becoming part of the problem, offer an alternative and become part of the solution.

Life is not fair. So, stop acting like it should be. Do your best to do what is right. If you suffer for doing good, so be it. When you can correct what is wrong, then do so. The world, your organization, you name it, owes you nothing. Life is not fair, so be it.

Pride. We all suffer from it. Never let your pride get in the way of doing what is right. We all lose.

Take initiative. Initiative with common sense makes a winning combination. Reward it. Encourage it. Live it.

Chain of command. There is a chain of command for a purpose. Follow it.

Fall on your sword. Go outside the chain of command only after it has ignored the issue and the issue is so important that it would cause life/death/injury to person or company. You may get hammered, so it better be worth falling on the sword for.

There is a fine line between "hooah" and stupidity. Hooah is defined as risky/dangerous/high payoff in this case. If your gut says about a situation, "Yes" and it is not ethically wrong, morally wrong, or going to get you seriously injured or hurt, then hooah! If you are not at least 60% sure of a positive outcome, then a "yes" decision would be stupid, not hooah! And if you can reasonably wait on whatever the decision is, then wait until 80% sure and run with it. Hooah!

Finally, never take things personally, even if they were meant to be personal. Look at the merit of what the person has to say. Is the person right? It is hard not taking an insult or constructive criticism personally sometimes, but you must. Learn from it and grow.

Chapter 27

Failure

Situation 1, Failure at work

My first airborne operation as a Jumpmaster (person in charge of exiting jumpers from an inflight aircraft) was a complete failure. I was previously warned not to pull a duty with the Primary Jumpmaster (Jumpmaster in charge) because that person was not up to standard. I ignored the advice and paid the price.

What happened? The entire Jumpmaster team was decertified because the Primary Jumpmaster had too many jumpers on one anchor line cable which was a safety violation as the cable could snap because of the extra weight of the added jumpers. If the cable snapped, then parachutes would not open and jumpers could die. It did not matter that the jumpers on the side of the aircraft I was on were safe to jump, there was an unsafe condition in the aircraft and no one jumped.

More importantly, what happened afterwards? Was I going to sulk in this failure or was I going to do something about it? From that day forward, I decided I was going to be the best Jumpmaster in the entire 82nd Airborne Division and nothing like this would happen again on my watch.

To make that happen, I sought out the most knowledgeable Jumpmaster I knew (a former Jumpmaster instructor at the Army school) and learned from him. I read everything I could find and I became a stickler for attention to detail (safety). I also performed Jumpmaster duties as often as I could, but always made sure the Jumpmaster team was competent and if not, corrected the team.

Within a nine month period I transformed from a failure to one of the best Jumpmasters because of hard work. People now came to me for guidance on running airborne operations and I had begun successfully training others for Jumpmaster school. I let my previous failure fuel my passion to become the best. I saw the failure as an opportunity and not the end of the world.

Situation 2, Failure at home

My high school sweetheart and I got married and eight years later we were divorced. It takes two people to make a marriage work and two people to make it fail. The divorce hurt not only us, but also our child. So I had a choice to make, do I blame my ex-wife or do I accept responsibility for my mistakes, learn from them, and move on?

I chose the latter. I read books about how to communicate better and the different love languages. I apologized to my daughter and my ex-wife for my failure as a father and a husband and I apologized to God also for this. I worked at being there for my daughter because of the responsibility I owe her and the love I have for her.

At work, I took a more personable view of my employees and counseled people how to learn from my mistakes so that their marriages could prosper. It was quite a wake up call for a few men who were heading down the path I had traveled.

Situation 3, Failure at sports

Babe Ruth, wildly famous for his 714 home runs, also failed to deliver many times. He had 1,330 strike outs! If you don't swing for the big one, you will never hit it.

Michael Jordan made many last second shots to win basketball games. He wanted the ball always, but what we don't remember is that over 20 times when he had the chance to make the winning shot, he missed. Yet, he still wanted the ball.

No one likes to fail, but every leader will fail. By nature of leading from the front, it is bound to happen. A misspoken word here, a wrong decision there, a forgotten meeting or family event, a missed shot, etc, you will do it. As mentioned previously throughout the book, own up to the mistake, confess the mistake to those affected by it, apologize, and move on.

Now, if you never fail at anything, then you aren't trying to become better. Failure is acceptable, if you learn from your mistakes. I admit that there are mistakes that you can't recover from, but those are pretty rare*. Even in those cases it is how one reacts to failure that determines the future. Turn the negative into a positive. Find a new way to achieve, examine yourself and the situation to see what you could have done better and will do better in the future.

Have you failed at anything recently? Are you accepting the failure or are you doing something positive to prevent the failure from happening again? Are you learning from your mistakes and growing personally and professionally?

Lastly, don't let fear of failure prevent you from trying. Get back on the horse and overcome the fear, otherwise fear wins and you lose.

*A distinction needs be made between mistakes and errors in judgment. Mistakes can be overcome by the individual; errors in judgment usually cannot. Mistakes are improperly doing a task, failing to do an assigned task, and you get the picture. Errors in judgment are doing drugs, beating your spouse, and are usually caused by character flaws. Errors in judgment generally require the individual desiring to change and getting help from others to change.

Chapter 28

Family First

Situation 1, Work first

"Not now, I just got home from work, can't you see that I am tired." or "I can't make the kids' games, I am too busy at work." and/or "I will be there," but never is. "Honey, I have to do this. How else can we afford to send the kids to school and live in this nice house?" Do these sound familiar? Does your whole life revolve around work? Does your daycare provider, school teacher, or other see your children and spouse more than you?

Don't get me wrong, work is important. You have a responsibility to your employer, but you have an even greater responsibility to your family. Your family needs you. You have the responsibility to raise your family, to instill morals in your children, and to nurture your spouse. Kids need their parents and spouses need their partners. When all is said and done and you are old and gray, what is going to matter to you more- I sure am glad I went to that board meeting or it was so great watching my daughter catch her first fish? Who is going to take care of you, your company or your children? When your children are grown, do you want hooligans or someone you can be proud of? You married your spouse because you loved that person, do you really want a divorce? Do you know how much divorce really hurts children?

What does family first have to do with leadership? Everything! To an organization, an employee with family problems is less productive and is more likely to have drug or alcohol problems.

Situation 2, Remember your family

Many of us focus so much on our jobs that our family and our faith takes a back seat. You made a vow to God to be there for your spouse and there isn't an expiration date on the marriage license. When you first started dating or got married, there was "Wow!" and fireworks of emotions. What happened? You grew apart. Why? Ask yourself the hard questions; drill down and find the real problem (See Chapter 2, Identify the Problem, Not the Symptoms) so you can fix it.

As long as the two of you are willing to work together, any problem can be overcome.

Situation 3, MBA and family

When I decided to get my MBA, I was working full-time, going to graduate school full-time, and being a single-parent father full-time. How did I manage to not neglect my daughter and make sure my daughter knew she was important to me?

Well, I decided to put her first. When I came home from work, from 6-9 PM was my daughter's time every night, except when I had study group once a week the first year. From 6-9 PM, Kathleen and I would eat, play, do her homework, watch TV, get ready for bed, read, pray, and put her to bed.

From 9 PM to whenever I fell asleep, usually around 10:30-11 PM, I would study. If I needed more time to study, then I took a vacation day from work and would study in the day time in order that I would be there for my daughter at night. On those study days, I would also take my daughter to school and pick her up from school so she could see I made time for her.

On regular work days, I would get her up every morning, make her breakfast, and drop my daughter off at my parents.

My daughter knew she was important. She was not second best. And as a second benefit to the way I managed my time, I was not burnt out and going to work everyday in a sleep stupor.

Situation 4, Bringing up the Past

> Wife: "John, I am mad at you. You left a mess in the basement and brought in those nasty car parts again."

> Husband: "I am sorry dear, do you mind if I wait 5 minutes, the game is almost over."

> Wife: "CLEAN it up NOW!"

> Husband: "Fine. Now, Honey, there is no need to scream. I will go clean it up now."

> Wife: Screaming, "You never learn! I had to tell you to pick up the living room last week. Then you forgot to get the groceries the month before that!"

> Is that fighting fair? No, it is not.

> The past stays in the past. Once you have forgiven a past problem, do not bring it back up. The other spouse will feel hurt, get angry, and tune you out. You must deal with the problem at hand and *only* the problem at hand.

Situation 5, Reoccurring problem

> Now, if it is the same reoccurring problem let's say of a husband forgetting to take off his shoes before coming into the house after a long day at work, then that is a different issue. Maybe the wife can lock the door, put a sticky note over the keyhole saying, "Please take off your shoes. Love, your wife" and provide him a chair to sit on. It won't be long before the husband will be cured. Generally, it takes 28 days to learn a new habit. Now, you have solved the problem without fighting or yelling.

Situation 6, Reoccurring problem, joint

Ok, let's say the two of you are having the same problem over and over and the two of you aren't working together to solve the problem, then you are also part of the problem (Go back to Chapter 1, Are You Part of the Problem or Part of the Solution?).

To remedy the problem for example, if the husband is messy, then the both of you need to agree on a way for the husband to correct the behavior. Maybe it is that the wife should ask the husband nicely to clean up and if he doesn't clean up, she tells him in a calm voice that it makes her feel unloved when he doesn't clean up his mess and would he do so now. The man should pick up the mess now and if he doesn't, then the wife throws the mess in the trash. The key thing is that the two of you have come up with a solution you both can live with and will correct the behavior that is causing the problem.

If you don't take care of your family first, you will not be able to do your best at your job and you owe your employer that. Sometimes family first means quitting a job that is taking you away from your family, not taking a promotion, or getting less pay so you can have more time with your family. Now, some of you may not put your job ahead of your family, but how about your sports/other hobbies? Any activity that puts a shadow over your family needs to be dealt with.

Are you taking time for your family? Does your family know how much you love them? When was the last time you listened to them about how you are doing? Is your job more important than your family? What about your hobbies? Now, ask your family these questions. Remember, their perception is reality, not yours (Chapter 7, Do As I Say, Not What I Do). Are you really meeting the responsibilities you owe your family? Are you fighting fair with your spouse/children when disagreements arise?

Conclusion

I have provided you with many insights of leadership that you can directly apply to work, home, and play. However, when all is said and done, what matters most is not what you did for an organization or yourself, it is the changes you made in people's lives. People are the lifeblood of an organization. Develop the people.

Furthermore, while making a difference in other peoples' lives is immensely rewarding, it should *not be at the expense* of your loved ones. Put your family first and your job second. Then your family wins and the organization wins.

Now, the hardest place to lead at is the home, because when you come home from work, you are still carrying the weight from your job. Leading at home takes the greatest amount of effort, but it also provides the greatest rewards to you, your family, and our society.

Find a balance between work, home, and play and then do what you think is right. If you do this, everything else will follow. I have found my strength through my faith in God and putting Him first in all areas of my life- first at family, first at work, and first at play.

So, in closing my personal thoughts on leadership can be summed up in this one sentence. *A leader that will not suffer to do what is right is a failure to what he believes in and a failure to all those who follow him.* Remember, leadership is a service.

I hope this book was helpful and sets you on the right path to being a better leader at work, home, and play. Remember, you will make mistakes. I do everyday. A great leader takes responsibility for the mistake, corrects the mistake, and moves on. You can do it!

Best regards,

Lee

P.S. You may be wondering why Family First was the last
chapter in this book. That doesn't make sense you say. Oh, but
it does for three reasons. First, for most people, family takes a
second seat to work. Secondly, by reading about Family First
last, it will be on your mind as my parting words of advice. And
third, you always save the best for last.

Recommended Reading/Movies List

Leadership Books

The Leadership Bible- God and John Maxwell. The bible is an awesome book in leadership by itself, but the insight John Maxwell adds to draw out these leadership principles is amazing.

360 Degree Leadership- John Maxwell. Well worth reading many times over.

FM 22-100, Leadership- It is an Army Manual and one of the best leadership manuals I have ever read. The first time I read it, I didn't think much of it. Then I read it again and again over the years and it is a fantastic book.

Parenting Today's Adolescent- Barbara and Dennis Rainey. This is a book about training your kids to be sexually and morally pure. The lessons are leadership in action. This is a must read for any parent.

The 5 Love Languages- Dr. Gary Chapman. No one cares how much you know until they know how much you care. Learn to speak the languages that let others know they are important to you.

MAX Out the Army, Navy, and Marine Physical Fitness Test- Lee A. Kind. If people have to be physically fit in your organization, you need to lead from the front. This book is great for all military and law enforcement personnel or anyone who wants to get in shape. My Soldiers begged me to write it, so I did. Easy to read and follow.

Managing the Obvious- Charles A. Coonradt, Jack M. Lyon, Richard, and Leonard Williams. Dated, but a great book. The obvious "common sense" is not obvious to most. Common sense is critical for the leader.

Making a Game of Work- Charles A. Coonradt. If you don't enjoy your work, you are missing out on a big part of life and you will not be an effective leader or worker in the long run.

Leadership Movies

We Were Soldiers Once- Tremendous movie that resonates leadership. There are scenes in that movie that make me cry every time I see it, because of the leadership demonstrated by heroic actions.

Facing the Giants- Tremendous movie about faith, loyalty, and leadership. A must see. I watch it once a month. Examples of great leadership abounds.

Gladiator- Leadership gone amuck and a leader that transforms others to do what is right.

The Ultimate Gift- A great story about the transformation of a selfish, angry man into a caring person that makes a difference. A great leader must be able to put others first.

Glossary

After Action Review (AAR)- An AAR is where one describes his performance- what went right, what went wrong, and what one thinks he can do better in that situation next time. An AAR many times also has a senior leader/observer who watched the event and gives feedback on what he observed, what you should have done, and what you can do better in the future.

Convoy Live Fire eXercise (CLFX)- A CLFX is where Soldiers shoot live ammunition at enemy targets from a vehicle (moving and stopped positions)

Differences between officers and non-commissioned officers (NCOs)- Officers are like top level executives, they are responsible for the overall organization and for the short and long range planning. Non-commissioned officers, on the other hand, are like front line management as they are in charge of the day-to-day operations. First Sergeants (1SG) and Platoon Sergeants (PSG) are NCOs that are in middle management and responsible for ensuring the front line managers are doing their jobs.

Jumpmaster- Person in charge of airborne operations. Maybe 5% of all the people on jump status are Jumpmasters. Jumpmasters inspect parachutes on jumpers to make sure it is safe to jump. Jumpmasters give jump commands and exit jumpers from aircraft while in flight.

Non-commissioned officer (NCO)- Enlisted Soldiers in the rank of sergeant and above.

Non-commissioned officer command positions and ranks from senior ranking to lower ranking:

Command Sergeant Major (CSM)- The highest ranking non-commissioned officer rank in a battalion and above unit. The CSM is the right-hand man of the Battalion and Brigade Commanders.

First Sergeant (1SG)- The highest ranking non-commissioned officer rank in a company level unit. The 1SG is the right-hand man of the Company Commander which is usually an officer in the rank of Captain.

Platoon Sergeant (PSG)- The highest ranking non-commissioned officer in a platoon and is held by a sergeant in the rank of E6 or E7.

Officer command positions and ranks from senior ranking to lower ranking:

Brigade Commander (BDE CDR)- Officer in the rank of Colonel in charge of 3-4 battalions which consists of 900-2,000 Soldiers.

Battalion Commander (BN CDR)- Officer in the rank of Lieutenant Colonel in charge of 3-6 companies depending on the type of battalion. Each battalion was made up of 300-1,000 Soldiers based on mission.

Company Commander (CO CDR)- Officer in the rank of Captain normally in charge of approximately 100 Soldiers in 3-4 platoons.

Platoon Leader (PL)- Officer in the rank of Lieutenant normally in charge of 30-60 Soldiers.

Ranger Challenge- A varsity sport for military ROTC that consists of constructing a one man rope bridge over water and crossing it, a 12 mile forced march with weapon and back pack weighing 35 lbs, weapons assembly/disassembly, land navigation, a Physical Fitness test, and a written test. The events are conducted over a two day time period. A team is made up of nine members and the top eight scores count.

ROTC- Reserve Officer Training Corps. A program offered at most colleges and universities for students aspiring to learn leadership and/or become officers in the military.